Home 10713 BiRch Tree lAne
    IndiAnapolis IN 46236
    Email Revmelvin @AOL.com
                        cell 869-7313
Melvin Hitchens - 317-826-3944

Interpersonal Communication Between Black Men and Women in the Family

by

Melvin Hitchens, Sr. ED.D.

Bloomington, IN Milton Keynes, UK

authorHOUSE®

AuthorHouse™
1663 Liberty Drive, Suite 200
Bloomington, IN 47403
www.authorhouse.com
Phone: 1-800-839-8640

AuthorHouse™ UK Ltd.
500 Avebury Boulevard
Central Milton Keynes, MK9 2BE
www.authorhouse.co.uk
Phone: 08001974150

First published by AuthorHouse 4/11/2007

ISBN: 978-1-4343-0803-0 (sc)

Edited by Dr. Yvonne Kirk.

Printed in the United States of America
Bloomington, Indiana

This book is printed on acid-free paper.

Forward

It is easy to write a book on the social ills of America today. Anyone who is an active member of society can see the impact these social ills are having on the "family." Many people report these ills, but few have taken on the responsibility of writing a remedy based on the prospective of a black man. Dr. Hitchens has taken on this insurmountable task by examining the problems of the black family and taking steps towards providing solutions. An ordained minister with a doctor's degree in education, he is well aware of the problems that assail the black family. Dr. Hitchens examines the state of the black family today, providing their history. He identifies the injustices the black race has suffered and the indelible mark these sufferings have left on the black family. He dissects and gives us an in-depth look at the black man and woman's relationship. Dr Hitchens goes a step farther in evaluating the father's relationship with his wife, his children, and society as a whole. What makes Dr. Hitchens' book so unique is that he is able to weave the past with the present, dealing holistically with the social ills while offering a guide for the black family. He calls on the black family to return to their religious roots where their foundation was God and the black church. This book will inform as well as educate.

ACKNOWLEDGMENTS

Today I am deeply indebted to those around me. Many persons have given me the inspiration to write this book. I wish to personally acknowledge my wife Gina, my daughter Gabrielle and my son Melvin. It is through the friendship of Rev .Tim Shelton, Rev Elaine Walters, Jeanna Knight, Dr. Kim White at Indianapolis University of Purdue University Indianapolis ,Dr. Ruth Lambert and Dr Lorain. Blackman that I was able to see the meaning and necessity of writing a book on the Interpersonal Communications between Black Men and Women.

Many thanks are also owed to my dear friends, Mr. Joe Kenny, Lloyd Howe, and Dr. Jim Dun, the department head of interpersonal communications and public speaking at Ivy Tech State College in Indianapolis, Indiana. Much appreciation goes out to the Rev. Peter Fenton and this congregation at First Samuel Baptist Church, and Dr. Yvonne Kirk.

Lastly a special thanks to my good friends Anthony Malone, Darwin May and Dr. Charles Ware, these three men serve as my mentors and inspiration.

Contents

Forward v

Acknowledgments vii

Introduction xi

Chapter 1 Interpersonal Communication between
the Black Male & Female in the Family.....................1

    The Unique Communication between Black Men
    and Black Women 4

    Gender and Cultural Differences 7

    Understanding Male and Female Relationships as
    it Relates to Stress 11

    The Black Male Love Needs..............................14

Chapter 2 Marriage and Relationships....................25

    "Self Evaluation"...28

    Principle Of Adaptation In Marriage................33

    Benefits of being marriage 35

Chapter 3 The Effects of Slavery in the Black
family..47

    Today's Affect of Slavery on the black women ..51

    Communication Style of a Black Woman 54

    Listening and Understanding for Black Men....55

    The Historical view of Relationship in the Black
    Family...58

Chapter 4 The Dilemma the Black Community
Finds Itself...61

    Code of the Streets..66

    The Community Must Go Forward 69

    Relationship Stage...70

    The Deterioration Stage 72

    Interpersonal Communication during Divorce..72

    Dissolving Anger in the Black and Marriage 78

    Main Points to Anger..80

Chapter 5 Understanding Self in Relationships 81

    Conflict Resolution from a Black Male's
    Perspective..86

    A Black man's Tools for Negotiation 89

    The Pain of Being a Black Man in America 90

    The Role of the Church in the Black Family.....94

Appendix (1) 103

Appendix (2) 105

Bibliography 109

INTRODUCTION

Our society has spent years discussing male and female styles of communication. Although much is discussed, very little is written. The ideas presented in this book are based on the author's experience and research while teaching in the classroom. This book provides an academic perspective to understanding the dynamics of communication styles of African American men and women. The book draws on the insight of black men and women as they have shared their love needs. Moreover society wants us to believe that there is warfare between black males and females. This is far from the truth; their styles of communication are different. This book serves as a celebration of the gender differences.

CHAPTER 1
INTERPERSONAL COMMUNICATION BETWEEN THE BLACK MALE & FEMALE IN THE FAMILY

Communication is to a relationship
What breathing is to maintaining life.
Virgina Satir

Most people would like you to believe that there is a warfare going on between the black woman and the black man. It may come as a surprise to know that there isn't one. However, misunderstanding and miscommunication occurs between the two, at times. In the family both parties, male and female, must understand their individual role of communication in the home. Each role is different, but critical in nature. The male role is to be a provider that takes precautionary measures to protect is family from danger. The female's role is different than her partner's role; she is to provide nurture for the nest. In front of the home where I reside, there is a large birch tree. It retains just the right amount of water for its daily use. At the top of the tree there is a bird's nest. The female bird comes daily to the nest to feed the smaller birds. Before she hatched her young, she moved through the air looking around the tree for the best smallest limbs to build the best nest for a rainy day. She seeks to minimize any danger, disaster, or unfavorable experiences that can cause calamity and endanger her young sheltered in the nest. The male's role in the family is serving as the pillow that creates the surface for stability.

The Black Family and Marriage

The family is the architect of our society. An architect is one who is involved with the design of buildings, complexes, or residences from their inception and finds solace only at its conclusion. Architects are valuable and responsible for the overall aesthetics of the building and the outer structure. This too is the role of the family. Not only does the family make sure things are aesthetically pleasing and safe within the home, but the family is also the building block of our society. The family unit introduces the newborn child to the world outside the mother's womb. It molds the young into the fine people they need to be. Through the process of teaching the child, the mother and father are able to impart values. They teach the child to respect adults and treat others the way the child wishes to be treated. The black family believes a person's credibility is critical to the structure of the family. If one isn't trust worthy in the family it is assumed there is simply a flaw in his or her reputation. Maybe this is because he or she has not been honest about something in the past. During family relationships we must always live life with much integrity seeking always to be upright and honest. It is clearly understood that families play a critical role in setting values in the life of children.

We must not forget that the black family is stronger and has more vitality than one cares to give it. In my personal childhood, we as a black family living in the south lived off our love for one another. Mother oftentimes challenged us as brother and sister not to forget the love God provided for us. She instilled a sense that if we tried to live that kind of relationship at home, that same kind of love would go with us everywhere we went. Mother would remind us of this principle by which we understand ourself and others. Such a love has to be relational. It must touch the lives of others everywhere you go, regardless of the color of their skin or their heritage. The black male and father in America loves his family as much as he loves himself. He supports the ideals of protecting, caring for and loving his family.

Lyndon B. Johnson conveyed in a speech in 1965 at Howard University:

> The family is the cornerstone of our society. More than any other force it shapes the attitudes, the hopes, the ambitions, and the values of the child. When the family collapses it is the children that are usually damaged. When it happens on a massive scale the community itself is crippled. Unless we work to strengthen the family, to create conditions under which parents will stay together, all the rest: schools and playgrounds, public assistance and private

concern, will never be enough to cut completely the circle to despair and deprivation.
(J.Deotis 1980 p. 24-25)

The black family is much more committed to the sense of kindness and respect than the media seeks to give it credit for. Black families have worked closely with the general public for the betterment of us all. Many black families consist of a strong group of people, seeking to utilize their strengths in maintaining a strong sense of identity for both themselves and their family.

The Unique Communication between Black Men and Black Women

Sometime when I consider what tremendous
Consequences come from little things.......
I am tempted to think......
There are no little things
Bruce Barton

The word communication originated from the Latin word "communi-care", which means "to impart or share knowledge with another person". To communicate with someone you must care about what is being said, otherwise, you will ignore what they are saying. Communication is really a process that consists of listing and speaking, and giving feedback. When listening, we stop and receive with our ears or decode the message that is being sent. The person speaking, usually the person that initiates the communication is the sender and the source of the communication.

Men communicate differently in a relationship than women. Contrary to what many may believe, in most relationships, men initiate the contacts and interactions more often than women. This is what probably led him to talk more during the onset of the relationship. In communicating with women, men tend to focus on topics to one they know more about or one that is less relational or more factual, such as sports, statistics, economic developments or political problems (Devito, 2005, p. 87). Black men communicate to show their expertise, to show their domination. According to a well known author Deborah Tannen, (Messages Building Communication Skills 2005 p.87), women seek to build rapport and establish a closer relationship and so use listening to achieve these ends. For example, women use more listening cues that will show the other person that they are paying attention and are interested. They provide eye contact, feedback and there is a constant flow and exchange of information. Both men and women have their "gender talk" which makes them different.

In my practice, I have noticed that females spend more time discussing their personal and domestic problems with other women. They sort out their problems together and work towards a solution. Whereas, men are less likely to discuss their problems with other men and are more likely to try to work on a solution on there own. According to the study of *Gender Differences in Communication* by Dr. Beth Vanfossen (2005), women interrupt more during conversations than men. Even if the man in question is the woman's spouse, she will choose whether or not to interrupt based on the situation. This study conveys to us that women tend to express friendships by complimenting one another and by sharing personal information. They also don't mind complimenting one another on their clothes or shoes, whereas, men usually do the opposite. They are not as eager to share their thoughts or problems. Most men perceive themselves as being weak if they discuss their problems with friends. Women don't have a problem releasing stress by sharing. Men, by nature, feel the need to handle things on their own. They like to fix things and make things better for others. Therefore, when a male hears a woman discussing a problem, he immediately begins thinking about how he can "fix" it for her and make things better for her. It makes him feel good if he can play "superman" in the situation. Men need to understand that women seek to show their closeness through *sharing* their problems. Sometimes, all a man needs to do is just listen to her problem and not try seeking a way to fix anything. "Just Listen." Don't try to give any advice at all.

Men communicate more effectively with one another around shared activities, such as at a basketball game or watching at a football game on a Friday night. Women usually communicate around sharing their feelings and providing personal support to one another. Again, even as I compare my daughter and my son, my daughter seems to self disclose more often than my son. My daughter will provide more intimate details in her conversation with me. Whereas, my son doesn't view details as important when he is in conversation with others. As previously stated, by contrast, men tend to come to aid of a situation by hoping to fix things an offer their advice while in the conversation. Women may discuss their troubles while in the beauty salon chair, or they may call up a good girlfriend. These are ways in which women in the urban community ventilate their concerns. People definitely help each other by listening and talking about life. Just talking to someone else helps clarify your own thinking. Men often use the barbershop chair as a way of clarifying their thoughts. In this setting there is definitely a listening audience, an audience that usually renders little judgment.

During the early years of life women are taught to look quiet, smile and seek to be pleasant and positive because that is what it means to be a young lady. Whereas, boys are expected to always be and look tough, rough and show more unevenness in their personality. In Dr. Vanfossen's study she suggested that during formal group meetings, men are found to capture and perceive information better then women. During the same meeting the female would ask questions so they could provide more input and direction to the discussion. Usually when a woman asks questions, she often has the answer in more than one way.

Gender and Cultural Differences

There is a gender difference between men and women other than their body make up. While observing conversations between my son and daughter the differences are apparent. When my daughter communicates she is more direct when it comes to letting her feelings be known. She finds no discomfort with voicing her opinion while giving orders at the same time. When she does this she always engages others into the conversation. This is true with most females-they have the ability to identify their feelings, whereas boys have a harder time identifying their feelings. According to Deborah Tannen (1994) men are more likely to use an indirect approach when they express weakness, reveal a problem, or admit an error or while expressing any emotions. However, they are more likely to be direct when expressing anger. The story below serves as example:

Mike comes home from work and finds that his wife and children are not home. His wife left a note saying that she was attending a function at the children's school. Although there are other issues in Mike's mind, He becomes upset because there is no dinner on the table and he wants to see his wife and children. Later, in a discussion with his wife, Mike seems angry. Instead of being upset about coming home to an empty house, Mike could be more direct about what is *really* bothering him. He is worried about his financial situation and is facing problems at work. Instead of confronting the problem, he blames his wife.

In a relationship, it is unfair and unproductive to play the "blame game". At all times be fair and determine who is at fault, even when it hurts to tell the truth. Describe your feelings and tell your partner what and who upsets you. Describe how you feel. Explain the origin of your disappointment. Talk about the discomfort of your disappointment. Try not to dwell on the conflict but instead, seek to discuss solutions. If you dwell on the problem, all you will have is a problem. Conflicted relationships tend to perpetrate themselves. They play off interactions and carry forward with a momentum that appears to have a life of its own. Sometimes, any intention on part of one person is predicated on the best prediction of what another person might do. If you are expecting a person to act deviously, you will prepare yourself for betrayal by cloaking your own behavior in deception (Kottler.J p.505).

When it comes to understanding both genders, there are two parts of communication that need be understood: message and meaning. This has to be understood by both parties holding dialogue. People often convey meaning to what is being said through their nonverbal communication, such as their smile, frown or gesture of the hand or eyes. Research makes it clear that women are more likely to express their emotions and use more non- verbal messages than men. They smile more than men even when it isn't appropriate. Men on the other hand seem to take things more serious. On an everyday bases, women communicate more happiness. Women communicate well with men who share their emotions. A woman's eye contact can tell you a lot about her intention. A five-second gaze into your eyes can say that a person is listening and the relationship is going in a positive or negative direction. For example, if you stare at a person with a frown you may be sending a signal that you are not interested in what they are saying or even, interested in the relationship. Eye contact is critical when communicating with others. It can enable you to psychologically lessen the distance between yourself and the person. For example, when you catch someone's eye at a party, although you may physically be far apart from one another, you become psychologically close (Devito p.124). Your nonverbal communication is what people depend on when your message isn't clear.

People can also send a message with a simple touch. The touch can be a good touch or made touch. When a father is disciplining his son it can be a bad touch for the son but a good touch for the father. Generally women communicate more through touch than men. Men typically subscribe to the notion of "control touch". This is generally a touch that supports good behavior and an attitude or feeling. An example is when a man pulls the child out of the way of harm or danger. This kind of communication is called tactile.

There are times when both parties engage in the silent treatment. Sometimes the spirit of silence can be used as a means of preventing miscommunication in a relationship. One party may use it as a way of keeping the peace. Additionally, this is used as a means of cooling down after a hot discussion before expressing any verbal pain and hatred. Sometimes both parties use silence as a strategy of defiant and uncooperative and annoyance, particularly when accompanied by a pouting. It is important to note that even silence is a way of communicating with your partner.

Understanding Male and Female Relationships as it Relates to Stress

What lies behind us and what lies before are tiny
Compared to what lies within us.
Oliver Wendell Holmes

In any relationship, differences are bound to arise. These differences lead to stressful situations that are a part of everyday life. Sometimes, we may feel as thought we cannot control the way in which we handle certain situations. In working through male/female relationships, we must be aware that men and women have different relationship and emotional needs. Both sexes define and gain a sense of self-worth in two totally different ways. A man's sense of self-worth is usually defined through his ability to achieve results, while women tend to define self-worth through feelings and in the quality of their relationships. These differences can create problems, because in difficult or stressful situations each partner does not always support one another's needs in positive ways.

In trying to understand and support the needs of each other, one must be mindful of the primary needs of each other. Each partner must also be mindful to show respect and learn to appreciate the needs and differences of each other. Men and women have six different love needs. How these needs are addressed in stressful situations determines the quality of the relationship.

Female Needs	Male Needs
1) Caring	1) Trust
2) Understanding	2) Acceptance
3) Respect	3) Appreciation
4) Devotion	4) Admiration
5) Validation	5) Approval
6) Reassurance	6) Encouragement

(The above love Needs are from John Gray, p.133)

In order for the relationship to flourish and develop, each of these needs must be met. Women must learn to trust, show acceptance of her partner as he is, show appreciation for his efforts, admire him for who he is, show approval for what encourages him and encourage him in his efforts. Men must learn to make his woman feel as though she is truly being cared for, is understood and respected. He must also show a genuine sense of devotion, validation and reassure her of her self-worth. When these basic needs are met, the love relationship flourishes and grows. When they are unmet, each partner begins to feel unloved. Unmet needs leads to stress and strife.

Without being aware of the inherent needs and differences of each partner, both partners make mistakes when handling everyday situations and upsets. Relationships fail and turn stressful because each person gives what is important to them instead of giving what is important for their partner. For example, women offer care when her partner wants to be trusted; she seeks to understand while he wants acceptance. Both sexes tend to make these and other critical mistakes.

A) Mistakes Men Make
1) Not attentive to basic needs
2) Does not listen and apply what is heard
3) Minimize the importance of her needs and feelings
4) Sets unrealistic expectations
5) Offers solutions and gives unsolicited advice

B) Mistakes Woman Make
1) Try to change and fix her man
2) Offer unsolicited advice
3) Openly corrects behavior; as if he were a child
4) Seeks to change behavior through manipulation and/or punishment
5) Becomes overly critical and complaining

The chart below represents a survey conducted at an African America church (First Samuel Baptist church located in Indianapolis, Indiana) with a membership of 800 people on the church roster. Forty students from a local college, Ivy Tech State College of Indiana, also participated in the survey. Each adult was asked to rank, on a scale of 1-6 with 6 the most important, which of the following love needs were most important in a relationship?

Male Response		Female Response	
Acceptance	111	Reassurance	221
Encouragement	157	Validation	224
Appreciation	128	Devotion	357
Trust	154	Understanding	265
Admiration	88	Caring	258
Approval	84	Respect	268

We will further discuss these findings in the next segments.

The Black Male Love Needs

*People who have good relationship home
is more effect in the marketplace.*
Zig Ziglar

For the African-American male the highest value in a relationship is encouragement. For him, this is the number one love need. I can understand the reasoning behind this love need. Today the media and society depicts him as a person who is less than a man. He is often looked upon as a misfit to the world. Therefore, he needs to receive encouragement to "never give up." Oftentimes women put their men down when they are angry. "You are just like your father. He "ain't" nothing and you "ain't" nothing either." Sometimes our words can be as a grenade, very explosive. Words such as these can lead to emotional abuse.

"Emotional abuse is considered by many to be the most painful form of violence and the most detrimental to self- esteem. Emotional abuse cuts to the very core of a person, creating scars that may be longer lasting than physical ones. With emotional abuse, the insults, insinuations, criticism, and accusations slowly eat away at the victim's self-esteem until he or she is incapable of judging a situation realistically." (Engel, 2002, p.277)

The black male needs to be inspired and encouraged with a spirit of hope. Today many people have a faulty worldview of him. He needs a cheerleader to inspire him to keep going.

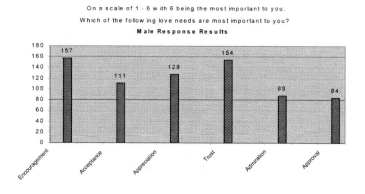

The survey also reveals that appreciation is critical for him during a relationship. We would like for her to appreciate him for who he is and what he has to offer as male, husband, father, and provider. The third most important love need for him in a relationship is trust. He needs her to have more confidence in him and his commitment to the relationship on a daily bases. He would like her to depend on him for future and contingent hope. The third love need for him in relationship is acceptance. Accept him as he is, don't try to change him. Sometimes women make the mistake of going into relationships seeking to change or fix a man as though he is broken and needs to be fixed. The fourth love need that is important to him is admiration. He would like for the female to admire him for the little things he does for her such as massaging her toes and back at night. He always wants to know he is making a difference in her life. "Doing little things for a woman is also healing for a man. In fact those little things will tend to heal his resentments as well as hers. He begins to feel powerful and effective because she's getting the care she needs. In this way, both are then fulfilled. (Gray, 1992, p.186) All of this leads to approval. He feels he is okay. He can say, "I am the man in this relationship."

The Black Female Love Needs

Doing more things faster is no substitute for doing the right things.
Stephen R Covey

For the black female, devotion is critical throughout the relationship. Whatever is going on in the relationship, she wants to know whether her partner is going to be devoted to her during the good times and the bad. For her, "to trust a man is to believe that he is doing his best and that he wants the best for his partner. When a woman's reactions reveal a positive belief in her man's abilities and intentions, his primary love is fulfilled." (Gray, 1992, p.135) Remember this is all about love and relationships and meeting the needs of each other.

The research shows that the second most important factor in a relationship for women is respect; she must be treated with high regard. Her mate must be courteous to her thoughts and actions even if he does not agree with her about an issue. When this happens he shows high regard for the relationship and for her. For her, this shows his sense of decency. We discovered that understanding was the third most important thing in a woman's life. She wants him to seek out more understanding when it comes to her needs in the relationship.

Women desire emotional gratification. For a woman, sex isn't everything. She would like her partner to talk about his feelings and she is energized in knowing that she is cared for, provided with a safe place to live, while having the financial security that is needed to create a happy home. For her, home is where the heat is and not sex. The fourth most important factor in a relationship for women, is caring. If her partner cares for her the way a man should care for a woman, she would gladly open up her heart to make him feel like a man. She is hungry to be cared for. She wants him to be the champion in her life. She never wants to feel as though she is alone in the struggle; the struggle called marriage and love. Lastly, women seek reassurance. They want the reassurance of knowing that the male is going to always be there in times of trouble. This reassurance restores daily confidence in the relationship.

Both sexes must realize that it is all right and often necessary to share expectations and negative feelings. However, this sharing should be done in love and genuine respect. Each partner must always be mindful of the needs and feelings of the other. We must always remember that differences of thought and opinion will occur, after all, relationships involve two totally separate and unique individuals. We must learn to embrace these differences.

In September of 2006, the government sponsored a conference to strengthen the black family. The conference was well received and strongly documented. Dr. W. Bradford Wilcox of the University of Virginia, one of the best educators and researchers in the field stated: "There's a culture causing the break- down of communication in relationships between black men and black women." This is his list of "cultural causes."

<u>Cultural Causes</u>
*Sexual revolution of 1960s and 1970s
* Broke connection between sex and marriage / commitment
*Undercut norms against premarital sex & sexual fidelity
*Men no longer obligated to marry women they impregnated (no more "shotgun" marriages)
*Popular culture
*Depiction of African-Americans, especially men, in a degrading manner

*Slavery didn't allow men to be "decent" husbands and fathers

*Slaves could not enter into enduring marriages

*Men could not provide & protect for their partners

*Men forced to endure long or permanent separation from their partner (Research from the black family conference, September, 2006)

*In the 1960s there were some social and structural causes we began to notice that effected black family life (i.e.).

*Relatively poor socioeconomic standing of black men compared to black women

*Since 1960s, black men's employment opportunities declined just as black women employment opportunities improved

* Now, there are 60 black female college grads for every 34 black male college grads

Sex ratio:

*50 young black men employed for every 100 young black women due to:

- Unemployment, incarceration, work in illegal economy

- Family structure: 80% of black boys can expect to spend a significant amount of their childhood years apart from their biological father

When we observe the statistics, they should call us to our knees. To effect social change in our community, the church community and the business community must initiate the proper educational programs to address the above concerns, so that we can minimize failure in the coming generations. In this regard we need to begin with being urged. We should use our creativity to come up with new ideas that would initiate action. We must hold one another accountable for our actions. We should try to see the good in people we deal with every day.

African-American leaders of today must become more street-wise and uncompromising, who have stopped looking to white America for answers. The Africa America community itself can do more than it has done in the past. Blacks today are better educated, better off financially, and have better jobs prospect than their parents, or even older siblings, but they are still not even to whites when it comes to job opportunity. Economically, blacks have made great gains, but they remain substantially worse off than whites in many parts of the country. Hurricane Katrina in New Orleans revealed that to all of us. We saw housing for blacks and whites still segregated, and the "white exodus" to the suburbs seems to be increasing de facto residential segregation in the central cities. When we speak of de facto segregation we mean that there is racial separation that often results from unofficial social patterns, as opposed to segregation imposed by law (de jure segregation) .

Slave Trade in America

The Southern States of Mississippi, Louisiana, Alabama and Texas, along the Gulf Coast were known to be slave trade states in the late 1700s and early 1800s. Many of the white slaveholders where cruel and brutal. During this time sugar cane plantations became plentiful, which increased the demand for owning slaves.

Purchase and sale of slaves linked New Orleans tightly to the large southern economy. Each year thousands from across the south passed through New Orleans' slaves pens, arriving and departing via boat or driven on foot, in chains. Slave trade was a daily, bloody, highly visible public affair of New Orleans. (Lavelle & Feagin, 2005, p.1)

Black labor was important to strength of the economic of the city otherwise it would have gone down in ruins.

In 1998 there was a Gallup Poll taken asking whether conditions between blacks and whites have improved or have gotten worse or stayed about the same.

Percent of people age 18 or older responding by race, age, and education, 1998

Population	Total	improved	stay the same	gotten worse	don't know
Men	63%	28%	5%	5%	
Women	63%	28%	5%	5%	
Black	42%	44%	11%	3%	
White	67%	24%	4%	5%	
Other	49%	39%	4%	8%	
Aged 18to 29	58%	30%	6%	5%	
Aged 30 to39	5%	35%	6%	5%	
Aged 40 to 49	62%	30%	5%	3%	
Aged 50 to59	62%	24%	6%	5%	
Not a high school graduate	61%	28%	3%		
High school graduate	64%	26%	7%		
Bachelor's degree	58%	30%			

Source: General social Survey Opinion Research Center,
University of Chicago: calculations by author

The above American attitude survey suggests to us that the race relationship between blacks and whites has improved greatly over the past two decades. But on racial issues we are still divided as a nation. Furthermore the research states on the average Negroes/ Blacks/African- Americans have worse jobs, income, and housing than white people. Do you think the difference is mainly due to discrimination?

Difference between Black and white Due to Discrimination, 1977 to 2002
(umber of respondent age 18 or older, and percent distribution by response, 1977-2002)

Date	Of respondents	Total	% Yes	% No	% Don't know
2002	907	100	33.5	63.4	3.1
2000	1,868	100	36.7	56.9	6.5
1998	1,864	100	35.1	58.5	6.4
1996	1,946	100	37.8	57.3	4.9
1994	1,968	100	40.7	54.2	5.1
1993	1,077	100	41.2	53.9	4.9
1991	1,020	100	39.9	55.7	4.4
1990	1,365	100	39.1	55.5	5.4
1989	999	100	39.8	55.5	5.6
1988	981	100	42.4	52.9	4.7
1986	1,464	100	43.6	53.6	2.9
1985	1,530	100	43.1	52.5	4.3
1977	1,347	100	39.2	56.3	4.5

Source: General Social Surveys, National Opinion Research Center, University of Chicago; calculations by new Strategist (From the American Attitudes the Fourth edition 2005 p.83).

There isn't an absolute reason for blacks have lower incomes than whites: much of it may have to do with job availability and access.

CHAPTER 2
MARRIAGE AND RELATIONSHIPS

Myth: "A great Relationship has nothing to do with Sex "
Phillip C McGraw

A good marriage does not come together because of a passionate interlude between two people, husband and wife. Nor does it come together because a man and a woman have taken a vow and have set aside a day that they call their anniversary. Good marriages are built on warm and loving relationships, which provide a principle of governing during their time together.

The ideal marriage should be intimately involved in all ways in love, righteousness, forgiveness, kindness, and pleasure. The word intimate is being used within the context of a confident, a close friend to whom you can love and appreciate enough to share your close feelings with during moments of stress. The particular experience we are concerned with is the wonderful, life-long love affair they have for each other. This unique relationship develops due to the respect they have for one another, and because of the appreciation they have for one another that grows out of love and kindness. The ideal marriage is provided for, because God is the center of the relationship. God means oneness. There is no separateness in God. God is God, all by God's self. God does not need someone else to make him God; therefore, God is oneness. God is complete all by God's self. God created mammals, day, night, and life all by God's self.

In marriage the relationship should reflect oneness, just as there is oneness in God. The couple does not need outside forces to make them complete, because what God has put together no man, or woman should be able to put asunder. When God does something, God does it for good. God breathed on it, so it is good. When God created this universe, God breathed on it and said it is good. Therefore, if God is the director of a relationship, it has to be a success; there has to be joy, pleasure, and happiness.

Yes, a marriage starts out to be the best it can be. Perhaps what sometimes happens along the way is that it loses its force and sense of direction. When traveling on a long journey, such as marriage, it is important to know which way to go and have the right guiding strength. Otherwise you may end up on a dead-end street. There must be a sense of purpose and direction in all relationships. The one that gives purpose and direction in life is God. Without God, the relationship will become stale.

Such a love should be deep and tender. It is a pattern for life upon which all things in a relationship are based. Their appreciation for one another should be based on their feelings, and by being kind to one another at all times. Kindness should be the trade of the relationship.

Marriage could be likened unto a life support machine. It must be taken care of daily. It must be provided for daily, so that in time of greatest need it will function to its greatest capacity. Otherwise, it will not work when we need it most. It will let you down. One must check each day to make sure that the machine's engine is workable and ready to function to its greatest capacity.

Love and relationships must not be taken for granted. Love must be nurtured and nourished with the right substances daily. The right substances will promote the right strength during moments of stress. An example of this point is a flower. It will grow under acute circumstances—lack of much water and little light—but ultimately it will become a dwarf, an atypically small plant which is stunted by malnutrition, lack of love, and affection. A marriage can experience this shock if one does not provide for it properly.

Perhaps one of the best ways of looking at the marriage relationship is to look upon it as a business contract, a covenant, which has been set up as a way of cooperating as partners. That is, we as two people will work things out for better or for worse, until death due us part. We will provide for each other and take care of one another, because of the relationship we have together. This relationship is founded on the openness to accept one another as we are. This openness is very much like a business agreement. As we all know in business, some obligations come along with the responsibility.

The first responsibility is to know your business enough to feel comfortable enough to provide for your customer, otherwise the company will not be around long. This too is important for any couple who seeks to be happy in a marriage. They must know one another enough so they can grow together in a positive way. Secondly, one must be creative enough to provide a wholesome environment for love and affection to grow. Thirdly, one must not plan to fail in the marriage endeavor. Moreover, fourthly, there should be a periodic review of the strengths and the shortcomings of the relationship. Otherwise, problems will creep furtively or slowly into the relationship. No relationship will survive without an inventory of knowing the gains and losses.

"Self Evaluation"

The following charts will help you evaluate yourself in a relationship or marriage. If you score 180-200, the relationship is healthy. However, if you do not score at least 100, the relationship is not in strong standing with both parties. Give your honest opinion regarding each principle in the relationship. For example, if there is little to no communication in the relationship, give a number from 1 to 5. If there is good communication, give a number from 6 to 10, 10 being the highest number you can score.

Communicates_____	Stubborn_____
Fair_____	Evil Most of Time_____
Negative_____	Responsive_____
Sensitive_____	Charming_____
Lovable_____	Helpful_____
Kind_____	Enthusiastic_____
Loyal _____	A Leader_____
Dependable _____	Determined_____
Indecisive_____	Willing to Work_____
Generous_____	Creative_____
Total_____	Total_____

If you find yourself easy to work with and not stubborn, creative and enthusiastic regarding your relationship, then the relationship has great potential for love and happiness. These are just a few keys of love. There has been no relationship that has had longevity without love and happiness and enthusiasm to keep it going for the sake of friendship and loyalty. Gary Smalley (1988,p.113) gives us several reasons people don't stay together during moments of "for better or for worse:"

1) They don't understand what the other person is saying and feeling.
2) Each must increase their eagerness for one another through feelings of passion. This doesnot always mean sex. It may be through warm feelings and knowing you are wanted.

3) Increased desire for one another.
4) Motivate your spouse when he or she is down.
5) Correct one another without defensiveness.
6) Give praise.
7) Encourage one another.
8) Assume household responsibilities each day.
9) Each must meet one another's material needs periodically. (Small & Gary, 1988, p.113)

Within a caring relationship there must be the practice of spending time together. Otherwise the relationship will not survive. Within this time there must be fun and excitement in the eyes of the two people involved. This time should be cherished by both parts. They should have an interest in the activities of one another. It is healthy for them to have their minds on the relationship. Out of this healthy feeling they will know they do care for one another and are greatly interested and involved. So, as a result, when they come together it is easy for them to talk and communicate out of love. Such a passionate feeling will provide strength during trying times. This is just the beginning of phileo love, love between a man and a woman.

Friendship will fade when neglected. Your relationship may need some repairs, but like a valuable house, restoration can take place if you care to invest the time and attention.

Always remember that friendship requires attention. It must have something to feed on and respond to. Ask yourself and your partner: What are we overlooking that could make our relationship better? If we are a bit bored, what are we doing to add zest to our friendship?

Any marriage can benefit from more phileo. Since this friendship is a living entity, it must constantly grow or it will begin to wither. Therefore you should think of tangible things you can do to help it grow. (Wheat & Perkerins, 1990, p. 113). This (friendship) too, can be looked upon as a blueprint for the ideal relationship we call marriage.

Marriage should not begin on paper first. It must begin in hearts, in the hearts of the bride and the groom. The groom and bride must not think they are in love. They must know it before the wedding takes place. Otherwise, there will only be a wedding on paper even after the minister pronounces them man and wife. A long-lasting relationship must be founded in love and appreciation for one another. Couples should spend quality time together talking during this time. Husband and wife should look at one another while talking. They should be close to sense the emotional feeling they have for one another. Talking allows them to see where they are in the relationship. It allows them to listen to one another and understand their feelings better and yet pay attention to one another, see how they respond under pressure while there are few people around.

There are five basic rules for communicating during these times:

1) Never repeat to anyone else the things your spouse shares with you privately.

2) Give your spouse your total enthusiastic attention and listen with interest while he or she becomes more comfortable with expressing himself or herself. Remember, expressing one's self it may not be as easy for your spouse.
3) Do not interrupt your spouse or jump to conclusions about what he or she is saying.
4) Acknowledge that you understand even if you disagree.   Repeat his or her thoughts and feelings back so that he or she is sure you understand. Do not let your disagreement sound like disapproval.
5) When you are sharing your thoughts, be careful never to sound as if you are heaping blame on your spouse. When either of you goes on the defensive, your communication goes too, and rapport must be re-established.(Wheat & Perkins, 1990, p.110)

During this quality time, silence can be an enemy. It can destroy the relationship so it is important to talk about one another's feelings, how the relationship is going, ways in which you can build on the relationship in a positive way. This is God's love as we read about it in the scripture. The Bible conveys to us, "to come and reason together, says the Lord" (Isaiah 1: 18). With this directive we discover God's love for us. "God commandeth His love toward us, in that, while we were yet sinners, Christ died for us." (Romans 5:8 KJV) Out of this agape love we discover God loves us. Within this context we find that the word agape takes on many forms, action, involvement, commitment and so on. Below are observations concerning agape.

1) Agape love means action, not just a benign attitude.
2) Agape love means involvement, not a comfortable detachment from the needs of others.
3) Agape love means unconditionally loving the unlovable, the undeserving, and the unresponsive.
4) Agape love means permanent commitment to the object of one's love.
5) Agape love means constructive, purposeful giving based not on blind sentimentality but on knowledge: the knowledge of what is best for the beloved.
6) Agape love means consistency of behavior showing an ever-present concern for the beloved's highest good.
7) Agape love is the chief means and the best way of blessing your partner and your marriage. (Wheat & Perkins, 1990, p.120)

Principle Of Adaptation In Marriage

"Love begins with a smile, grow with a kiss and ends with a teardrop."
Anonymous

Knowing who you are as you go into a marriage is important to the life of a good marriage. When one gets married, there are sudden changes he or she can expect due to the life adjustment of marriage. In marriage, we bring our whole self to the relationship-good and bad. These experiences can enhance and strengthen the life of the marriage if both people are aware of their life and past experiences.

In marriage and family life there are key elements which can help the relationship:

1) Control or the lack of it. Each person comes to the relationship with rules and principles they were taught as a child. With such rules come limitations-knowing how far they can go in a relationship for it to be destroyed or strengthened. Each person's parents may have taught them differently about life and the limitations which come with them to bring about peace and harmony. What one person may consider to be a threat, the other may consider only as a way of expressing conflict. As long as he orshe gets what they want, things will be okay with them.

2) Selfishness. "Most new couples have at least some difficulty in learning to live unselfishly in the intimacy of marriage. Selfishness impairs all relationships in home life, including the sexual."(Wheat & Perkins, 1990, p.63)

In a marriage neither partner should thrive on selfishness. Otherwise, it will destroy all levels of communication. Sex should not be used as a way of getting even or holding back because the relationship is experiencing some tension. This could be one of the signs of difficulty young couples may experience during the first few years of marriage. The first year people are just getting to know one another, their way of communication, and their way of thinking.

Marriage should rely on two things—love and feelings from the heart. If feelings from the heart are honest and fair, the relationship will manifest the same status in the life of the family. Before getting to the point of marriage, however, those involved must know what they want, know themselves, and know what they have to offer to an authentic relationship which will be valid to the environment we call love. Before entering into marriage, a couple should do or ask the following question:

1) Is he or she willing and ready to follow his or her heart at a gut level for the sake of love and the relationship. Many times in a relationship one will not have all the answers to the challenges that many occur. However, if he or she follows their gut level of understanding, often, the right decision will be made.

Benefits of being marriage

In most cases both persons in a marriage, mother and father benefit greatly from being wedded to each other. Children that grow up in a household with both parents often receive daily love and disciple from both parents. Because both parents are in the home, the child can communicate with both about his or her problem. The child has immediate contact with both parents rather than having to wait for the weekend to visit mother or father at their separate apartments on Saturday. This can lead to multiple successes. Children that live with both parents experience less stress in school and perform better than those that live in separate households. It is also critical for children to see fathers expressing their love within the home.

Children with co-habiting parents have outcomes more similar to children living with single (or remarried) parents than children from intact marriages. In other words, children living in =co-habiting unions do not fare as well as children living in intact, married families. For instance, one recent study found that teenagers experience more behavioral, emotional, and other difficulties than teenagers from intact, married families even after controlling for a range of socioeconomic and parenting factors. (Institute for American Values, 2005, p.13)

Children that come from stable households function better in society, because mother and father became their first role model in life. Other benefits:

- Children who live with there own two married parents enjoy better physical heath, on average, than do children in other family forms.
- Parental marriage is associated with a sharply lower risk of infant mortality.

- Marriage is associated with reduce rates of alcohol and substance abuse for adults and teens.
- Married people, especially married men, have longer life expectancies than do singles people in similar situations.
- Marriage is associated with better and lower rates of injury, illness, and disability for both men and women
- Marriage seems to be associated with better heath among minorities and the poor. (Institute for American Value, 2005, p.11) Marriage is the most power institution there is on earth. It can be one of those things that keeps us civilize on earth.

The Benefit of Having a Father in a Girl's Life

It was a late Wednesday evening, and I was in the car with my daughter and her girl friend. While driving, my daughter's girl friend, quiet in the back seat, suddenly came to life asking my daughter one of the most important questions of that week. "Are you going to the school big party of the year?" We will arrive there in a limousine. We all must pay five-dollars to rent the limousine." My daughter paused for a minute and said, "Why should I ride in a limousine when I have my father to pick me up and take me where I want to go?" After hearing that conversation I realized my daughter knew that her father would always be there in her life when she needed him. She knew what the future would be like on a daily basis by, "Having a father in her life to help her to develop confidence in herself and femininity; that helps shape her styles (personality) as the first man in her life." (J. Barras, 2002, p. 55) Mothers in a girl's life help set the standards, but a father helps set the norm and values. Norms are those things we accept as right and fair in a relationship, and guides your standards. They help you set standards for achievements, relationships, life in general. In the future my daughter can have a healthy interaction with the man of her choice. Men communicate with their daughters differently than with the other women in their relationships. Often in a relationship men want what they can get out of it, but women are often looking for love and affection, hoping that he will show deep feelings for her. A father can explain to her the terrain of a man. This isn't sometime mother can do adequately. "The absence of a father in a young girl's life predicts her difficulty in adjusting to married life, thus ensuring the continued increase in divorces," said California psychologist Judith Wallerstein, (1995) who studied the plight of children of divorce parents for twenty-five years. (Barras, 2002, p.54) The father is the first male in the girl's life who can teach her how to bond through love and caring. He can teach her to share her world, go beyond her own boundaries and do so with great confidence. During the girl's early years it is important for her to hear from her father that she looks cute in that dress. Finally, he can teach her how to behave properly in society when around men.

I have a teenage daughter who is confident knowing that if she runs out of school supplies at 8 o'clock in the evening, she will have them in her room the next morning. Just going through this experience, I am able to present a model of a strong male to her. She is able to see things like this and know what she wants in a man in the coming years.

According to the National Fatherhood Initiative, (2005,), girls who grow up without a strong role or father tend to have a earlier sexual appeal for the opposite sex. Sometimes sex isn't enough. Fatherless girls develop an obsession with having a baby. A baby is a defense against loneliness, against abandonment. "In our fantasies we try to believe that man we have chosen to love us will not leave-as our father did." (J. Barras, 2002, p.70) As result there is a strong possibility she can grow up with hostility toward men, because she has been disappointed by a man in her earlier life.

Girls who grow up without their fathers tend to:

1) Have marriages ending in divorce.
2) Have children out of wedlock which leads to an increase in poverty.
3) Build less wealth over their lifetime.
4) Co-habit as couple- boyfriend and girlfriend.
5) Experience material hardship early in life.
6) Marry a man with fewer economic benefits.
7) Have a higher chance to drop out of school and not attend college.
8) Reduces the likelihood that her children will graduate from college.
9) Increases the likelihood of suicide and depression in her life.

10) Have a greater chance to experience substance drugs early in life.

11.) Girls and boys raised in single- parent families are more likely to engage in delinquent and criminal behavior.

Mistake Fathers Make with Their Daughters

A) Assume it is their job to fix thing in the daughter life

B) Not being involved in the day-to-day details of her life

C) Not allowing her to talk about her feelings

D) Not bonding with her

Girls are one of America's most precious commodities, they are worth more than silver and gold. One day a special "girl" I knew, grew up to become a woman and then my mother. One day she placed her feet into the doctor's stirrups. They said push, push, and I was born.

Everyday, I teach my daughter she is worthy of any man. When she does select a man in her life, he must be better or at least equal to her father. He must be a man.

The Role of a Father in a Boy's Life

If we fail to instruct our children in justice, religion, and in liberty,
we will be condemning them to a world without virtue, a life in the twilight
of a civilization where the great truths have been forgotten.
Ronald Reagan

The father is the one that provides hope and encouragement. He is like a coach whose team is trailing at halftime. The father's job is to instill hope and provide direction. As with a coach when the father sees that something is not working, he must call time-out and create a different game plan. The father should be the one in the family that teaches the son what it means to be loyal as a man. A father teaches a son that when you promise someone that you will complete a task, follow through on the promise. Complete the task with dignity and grace. The father should be the source of love and comfort to his children and in all cases model of self-discipline and self-pride.

I must admit that there have been times that I have failed as a father. I remember a time when my son was in middle school and in full gear of experiencing the adolescence years. He was not what most people would consider to a bad child, he never got in trouble with the law and never stayed out late or got into any trouble at school. He always managed to associate himself with a group of children who had similar "good" habits. In these regards he was a "good" child. What irritated me was the fact that he did not display any type of work ethic. He would half do his homework and what he did complete he would lose it in either his school locker or his backpack. He would never take the initiative to do things that needed to be done. In short he totally was not a responsible person and was totally unaware of the consequence of his irresponsibility. One particular day the consequences of his irresponsibility did not rule in his favor. I plowed in to him with two belts. As a father I put more than prayer on him. I so wanted for him to become a responsible person that I allowed my anger to become uncontrollable. I wanted him to understand that in order to grow up and become a man means that as a boy you must become responsible for your actions and realize that consequences come along with inaction. Everyday I tried to instill in him the importance of becoming a self-starter.

Today in looking back I realized that I tried to instill these values in him through a management process. I now realize that instead of relying solely on a management approach, I should have used a consultative approach. Instead of trying to manage his behavior and force support I should have asked if he needed help, and if he felt that together we could help him to become more responsible for his actions. I should have let him suffer more of the consequences instead of always "balling" him out by yelling what he should do and managing him until it was done.

One thing that I did right and I tried to do often was I sought pleasure in the things he did well and gave him must praise for those things. This is a critical role that father must play in a boy life. Giving him the praise and positive reinforcement he needs to continue in life. " Like flowers under rain and shine, children blossom and bloom under recognition and praise." Catch them doing something good and when you do, give effusive praise! When they make mistakes or fall short, help them accept responsibility for it and then praise that acceptance to the point that their pride in their self

–reliance outshine their concern over the shortcoming (Lina & Eyre, 1993, p.93) The father must set good examples for their sons. One day I was driving my son to school and I ran a stop sign. I remember saying to him when you start driving, "don't do what I just did." I immediately realized that I was setting a bad example and apologized for my failure.

There are times a father must recognize some of his shortcomings before his son. A good father must teach by good example and must model good behavior while teaching the example. Today if anyone would talk to my son Melvin II about what it is to be a man, he would say that my father modeled the behavior that he wanted me to display.

The Consequences of a Boy not having a Father in His Life

Chances are greater that:

1) He will not complete high school
2) He will be enticed by drugs easily
3) He will have sex early, becoming a father after adolescence
4) He will not be encouraged to form a traditional family
5) He will not have a full understanding of himself and his history
6) He will become prone to bad choices early
7) He will become an abandoned father or abandon his children

8) He will not have an understanding of basic norms and values of society
9) He will be likely to engage in delinquent and criminal behavior
10) He will have an increased likelihood of suicide and depression in life

The Mistake Fathers Make with Their Sons

A) Not bonding with them and just talking with them
B) Being too critical
C) Demand too much, too fast. This can frustrate the son.

The Relationship Between a Boy and His Mother

It is exciting to observe the relationship a boy has with his mother. Mothers have a unique way of communicating with the son. She has a keen way of initiating conversation with him. She knows how to probe his adolescent mind. Boys find themselves more and more cooperative with moms. Mothers seemed to have been blessed with a spirit of patience, a gift that most men do not possess. This patience is eagerly shared with her sons. Perhaps the Lord has blessed women with this gift and it begins with the child birthing process. Mothers have to carry their unborn children for nine months and watch the slow processes of life forming from within. Mothers are passionate people, while fathers tend to me more critical and judgmental. Mothers have the ability to wipe away the tears. This innate spirit often leads the mother to be the nurturer in the family. Throughout life, regardless of age, a son wants his mother's emotional support and approval. He finds it easier to take his serious problems to his mother. He will often confide in his mother his problems relating to girlfriends and other issues relating to life and relationships. Erik H. Erikson (1968), a noted psychologist suggested that a boy never wants to lose the connection with his mother. She is the bedrock of his life. Boys often place their mothers on a pedestal, because there are times when the father may too critical of the son. " A boy may find it easier to defy his mother, because she is more sympathetic, less threatening, and physically smaller than his father. Or he may see her as an all-powerful woman and worries about being absorbed by her. " (Caron, 2004, p. 42) Mother is the lifeblood of our society.

CHAPTER 3
THE EFFECTS OF SLAVERY IN THE BLACK
FAMILY

There can be no friendship without confidence
And no confidence with integrity.
Samuel Johnson

Since slavery the black family has been cast into a negative light. It has been said they are lazy and don't want to work or get out of bed. All they want to do is receive a monthly welfare check from the government. Some have even gone so far as to say if you are going to get something done you've got to have a white man around, otherwise it will not get done right. To some degree many people believed that after slavery, even some blacks. Slavery caused blacks to believe that they are less capable then they are. This was a deliberate strategy of the slave master during the 1700s to promoting racial superiority, and the belief that they have a higher rank in life than any other group of people. So consequently the white man's work will always surpass the work of any other ethnic group. Because he is white, there is a constituency built in his genes when it comes to doing a job right. Some people (blacks) insist that whites are not held accountable to the same degree as blacks, because in the end they will achieve there goal in whatever they set out to do.

In the United States of America slavery plays a significance role in the economic grow of the country. In America, the economy of the south , where "Cotton was King", was built on the backs of slaves. Slavery helped in aiding the building of the railroad system all across the country. There was a time when we did not have the railway system we have now. The railway helped us to transport cotton, sugar and tobacco from farmer during the harvest time of the year, starting in early summer. April to November, much of the exporting of goods were from the United States of America to the Caribbean countries and Africa.

Slavery in the United States had important political implications. During the westward   expansion ˙ of slaver during the early and mid-1880s, Northerners feared that the South would   gain control of Congress if the West territories entered the Union as slave states. Attempts by   the North to exclude slavery from these territories angered the South and helped bring on the American Civil War in 1861. (Bales, 2004, Wikipedia Free Encyclopedia)

During slavery women and children where forced into prostitution for monetary reasons to help balance the master's monthly income. Slaves received harsh treatment daily and required high levels of supervision, because they always wished to escape the harsh punishments of slavery. There where at least four types of slaves. 1.) There was the domestic slave who cooked the food and cleaned the house for the master 2.) There were those who did hard labor like working in the field picking cotton. 3.) There were some who worked in the mineral mines extracting coal from the earth, and 4.) There were some in the military who fought for their country. Slavery was used for anything that would strengthen economic development of the country. They where used for the cutting of the grass around the plantation, baby sitting and cooking. As a human being your sole purpose for existing was to provide labor service for the owner of the plantation. You were their legal designate, property by law.

Even today slavery continues to have a tremendous affect on the black male family.

1) It has aided men to produce children with out the resources to take of them.
2) It has fostered the idea and pattern to simply abandon his family when tough time comes.
3) It has also fostered the idea that he does not need to know the mother of this child.
4) The assertion was made that he did not support the notion of being a responsible man, however he was forced to leave after impregnation of the mother of this child.
5) It did not let him feel the stability and dominance of being a man in the household.

6) He only was known as a good breeder and not as a man.

Patterson, (1998, p. 42) quoting the well known anthologist and reproductive specialist and researcher Jane B. Lancast who stated:

> Under conditions where the most men can offer is their good genes and fit physical condition, women should be more interested in indications such as handsomeness, masculinity and athletic ability, but not particularly in youthfulness, because male reproductive potential deteriorates much more slowly and is not limit by menopause.

> The ultimate goal on the plantation for the male was to produce as many children as possible so there could be more help around the plantation. This was the only away males could show his manhood.

> In the absence of any other meaning ways of expressing manhood, becoming a progenitor would have acquired special. Many slave men who were unattached or who were forced to live away from partners they did not entirely trust, impregnating as many women as possible would have been the most rational reproductive strategy.
> (Patterson, 1998, p.43)

During this time there was very little dating, mating was more important. Certainly slavery had has a great effect on the black today.

Today's Affect of Slavery on the black women

1) It placed her on the pedestal when come to the family and it placed the man below the pedestal.
2) She became the MVP of the family, (Most valuable player) in the family, because of her sustaining role to in the family.
3) It taught her not to defer or trust him.
4) It gave her the notion that she should be responsible for everything financially the car, house, children, dental insurance, etc.
5) It fostered the notion it is okay to mother a number of children outside of marriage.
6) It fostered the notion it is okay to have different children with different last names.
7) It taught her that she can do bad all by herself.
8) It taught her the value of sacrifice in life. She had to make vital decisions to keep the family together. It was important for the African America female to adhere to sexual norms of the day, whatever that might be, at that time during that day.
9). It taught her how to fight for her family and not just "cut and run," as soon as she realized she was being attached. Most slave women adhered to stable sexual norms, as did, in all likelihood, that minority of male slaves fortunate enough to find compatible spouses on their own plantation

A substantial *minority* of slave women must have had multiple partners and led more freewheeling sexual lives, and it must have been these women who met the sexual needs of the *minority* of slave men who were either completely without regular partners or were forced to stay away from their "abroad" for long periods of time.". (O.Patterson, 1998, p.36)

The agony and torture that both genders experienced was much more than hazing, it was pain to the core. Carol Stack pointed out to us that it would be accurate to believe slavery has effected relationships between black men and black women. When a black woman experienced marital turmoil in her life she undoubtedly turned to her mother. "Because men had no legitimate ties to, or right in their female partner, they tended to emphasize the ties they were certain of, namely those they had acquired by "blood" through their mother."(Patterson, 1998, p.34)

Slavery fostered and created deep-seated tension between the man and female. It bred distrust in gender relationships, especially the male. This is where the relationship crisis began between the two. Obviously, under the great strain and compulsion of slavery it was difficult for him to process this emotion and feeling. He never got a chance to really cool down while under the pressure of slavery. He was only known for potentially, for his sperm and being the strong buck. He could not stand up for his family nor even protect them. There was a disagreement between he and the white master, one he could never define. There was never a time when he could state or represent his feelings within. There were few available options for him other than death. This is how a lot of black men feel today. There wasn't a time of negotiation for him. Negotiation is the keyway meaning a disagreement can be resolved. This is true for all kinds of disagreements at all levels in the family and in working with friends. Both parties, male and female must understand you can't negotiate a conflict, because angry people are emotionally stirred up to the conflict and often, can't sit down together and be reasonable about things. In life anger must be taken out first and then we can go ahead and deal with disagreement. Today's black women must first, understand the struggle, otherwise there will be more conflict. John Gray's (1992) *Men Are from Mars Women are Venus* said, "They communicate differently." For example, consider what he said:

> Women generally do not understand how Martian (men) view coping with stress. They expect men to open up and talk about their problems. Venusians (women) do. When a man is stuck in his cave, a woman resents his not being more open. She feels hurt when he turns on the news or goes outside to play some basketball and ignores her.

> To expect a man who is in his cave instantly to become open, responsive, and loving is as unrealistic as expecting a woman who is upset to calm down immediately and make complete sense. It is a mistake to expect a man to be

in touch with his loving feelings just as it is a mistake to expect a woman's feelings to always be rational and logical. (Gray, 1992, p.33) The black male's and female's struggle isn't from Venus or Mars, but from their history. We must not forget the black experience is black history. It is the black "soul" the pain and joy of reacting to whiteness and affirming blackness. Black history is the record of the joy and the pain. It is those experience that the black community remembers and retells...(Cone, 1970, p.60) It is this experience that black man feel and cry silently.

Communication Style of a Black Woman

Lean to listen. Opportunity could be knocking at door very softly.
Frank Tyger

Black women communicate a lot with their hands and are apt to use more eye contact when talking than men. They may often interject the words uh-huh" or the word "yeah" when talking to let others know they understand what is being said. Whereas, a man usually gives very little cues to let you know he is listening while you are talking to him. Black woman don't mind taking charge of a situation quietly. Here are some cues women use to alert you she is willing to do so.

1) Putting their hands on their hips.
2) They start moving their neck and then become twice as animated filled with vigor.

3) She may start rolling her eyes while you are talking, this is usually a cue that she isn't happy with something you have said.
4) There is a psychological change that could even take place during this time. Her eyes may become larger and she just may become louder in her presentation.

Not long ago I had a black woman say to me. "If I can drive this damm ship, why do I need a passenger that will weigh my ass down?" Black women communicate in the family in a "frank" way. Often they are straightforward and very forthright, however, such words can be damaging to any relationship. There is no evidence to show that these differences represent any negative motives- desire on the part of men or women .Neither does it suggest that one is superior over the other. What the differences reflect is how men and women have been socialized.

Listening and Understanding for Black Men

We are what repeated do.
Excellence, then, is not an act, but a habit.
Aristotle

As a black male my wife has said to me very often, "you don't listen." She always equates not paying attention to not listening. Women always want men to show their emotional ties to their conversation while listening to them. There are times I may not be looking her in the eyes, but still listening. At such time I do more active listing. In a marriage men seem to do more active listing. Always seeking a way to reflect back on what is being said. He knows that he will be tested on whether he was hearing the necessary points that are important to her feeling and emotions.

When dealing with a women of color one must be objective; be especially careful not to lead her in the direction you think she should go. A man should ask questions to strengthen his understanding of what is being said, then and only then should he paraphrase what is being said. An example, of this could be:
"Mary is this the way I hear you say this?…..…………
"Mary this is the way I am somehow hearing you. Am I correct?"
"Mary how can I get a better understanding of what is being said? Can you help?"
"Mary help me out? I am not "feeling" it. Give it to me again?"

- In this context paraphrasing means one should state in their own words what you think the other person is saying to you, and how you understand what is being said. Paraphrasing gives you the opportunity to echo the other person thoughts. In paraphrasing, Thomas Gordon (1975), a great support writer said: "Be especially careful to avoid sending solution messages." Solution messages tell the person how he or she should feel or what he or she should do. There are four types of solutions messages and you'll want to avoid them in your active listening. They are:

1) Ordering messages- "Do this…..Don't touch that…."
2) Warning and threatening messages- "If you don't do this, you'll …if you do this, you'll.."
3) Preaching and moralizing messages- "People should all…… We all have responsibilities…"
4) Advising messages- "Why don't you…What I'd do is……"
   (Devito, 2005, p.83)

Conversations at every level need to be focused explicitly on increasing understanding and communication.

When having a significant conversation with people we love and cherish, it important to get a clear understanding of each other's expectations. Always listen to what is being said with the intention to respond later on. Don't listen with the intent as though the conversation never happened, because the other person will find it difficult to meet your needs. Sometimes a person needs to know what is important to you, and what conditions you are working under. Many times people expect you to come up with the answers not a question.

We definitely need to foster leadership especially among our black men, because leadership knows no levels. I think that conversation at every level needs to be focused on and explicit about increasing communication between males and females. We need to be persistent and consistent in terms of what the conversation is all about. The way to get better in communication is through collaboration-which again addresses that problem of lack of coherence.

The Historical view of Relationship in the Black Family

> *There is no real excellence in all this world*
> *Which can be separated from right living.*
> **David Star Jordan**

Historically the black family has always subscribed to the principle of fairness. The writings of Dr. Martin Luther King are a prime example of the social consciousness they have upheld over the years. In history there have been personal and collective problems that have brought on the present crisis today, such as racism, the lack of a quality education, and the pressures of social evils permeates society. Dr. King, in this writings sets the foundation the African American needs to subscribe to when it comes to interpersonal communication and how to get along with others.

Let us now move from the practical to the theoretical "why": Why should we love our enemies? The first reason is fairly obvious. Returning hate multiplies hate and adds deeper darkness to a night already devoid of stars. Darkness cannot drive out darkness; only light can do that. Hate cannot drive out hate: only love can do that. Hate multiplies hate, violence multiplies violence, and toughness multiplies toughness in a descending spiral of destruction.

Another reason why we love our enemies is that hate scars the soul and distorts the personality. Forgiveness does not mean ignoring what has been done or putting a false label on an evil act. It means, rather, that the evil act no longer remains as a barrier to the relationship. (M, L, King, 1963, p.42-45)

However, good communication is the key in any family situations. Otherwise, there will be chaos on every level. We all must communicate so that we can connect and develop the love of God in our lives, and for the good of all humanity. Perhaps in this discussion we should embrace some of the views of another contributor in life of African American History, namely Marcus Garvey. Garvey believed that the Negro or black American should become more of an independent thinker and seek to solve his own communal problems and not depend on white America for any answers. He "created a new validation of everything black or Negro. He created a military organization which was to be vanguard of the African army and he organized a corps of Black Cross Nurses. He invented honors distinction which caused the Negro to feel that he was a part of a great cause. He set up stores and restaurants and started a project for a fleet of steamships that would bind the Negro in America to Africa." (Franklin, 1957, p. 121) Garvey, born in Jamaica in 1885, presented the self-sufficiency model to blacks in early 1900s.

CHAPTER 4
THE DILEMMA THE BLACK COMMUNITY FINDS ITSELF

*There is more at stake in the struggle for
Survival than mere physical existence.*
James Cone

Today the problem with the African American community is our every behavior has been a distraction. Gang violence is permeating our community at an alarming rate, one out of five crimes that take place in the United State is committed by black youth, and it is usually black on black crime. We must teach our children to become creative in the market place, which can led us to an invitation to construct the future through innovation and action. The community as whole must come together to discuss the strength, successes, hope, values and dreams of African American youth.

We must not forget that what is happening in our inner cities is our problem as people, and as nation. It is a microcosm that is taking place in our home and in our schools. There is a breakdown in communication in the home with parents. There is a breakdown in communication in schools with the teachers. These breakdowns lead to a breakdown in the ability to communicate in the streets with one another. I mean, it's almost as if we've replicated the one in the other. There must be some breakthrough in leadership whereby we can see the light. In history the black church was known to be the catalyst for social change. Now, they have become the regulators in the community. They have been known to regulate political policies and have ceased to be the service center for the black community. A service center is place that makes people better. It enables people to focus more on providing for the needs of those needing help in getting along in everyday life. We have done little in enhancing the social and interpersonal skills of the people. Dr. Wilcox's research (2006) states that Black (and other) churches do not:

- Provide clear consistent messages on sex and marriage.
- Both issues are taboo, because of traditionalism and demography
- Focus on other issues(e.g. community building) This helps to explain why black

Churches can not supply "silver bullet"

Black churches do foster a code of decency that encompasses hard word and sobriety.

This code has an indirect positive effect on black relationships and the odds of marriage among African Americans. As you can see the church and religion must seek to speak to the whole needs of the community when it comes to the development of interpersonal skills, relationship building, and getting along with one another.

The crime rate in the mid-size cities has sky-rocketed over the last ten years. American youth are out of control. "The new violence is also a part of an old problem, the aftermath of the crack epidemic of the '80s and 90s, which sent mothers and fathers to prison. The kids of those parents who are incarcerated are those who are committing the gang violence on the streets. The bitter kids are now the gang members we see today."(Jackson, 2006) These youth's lives are very unsettled. According to the CBS New report October 17, 2006, police offices around the country are over-stretched and strained when it comes to youth crime. Police departments everywhere are faced with this epidemic. The nations FBI report stated in 2005: The murder rate in St. Louis and Cleveland has increased by 8.7 percent, while the rate for bigger cities like New York, Los Angeles and Chicago increased by only 0.6 percent. "The number of murders in Marion County, (Indianapolis, Indiana) is nothing to brag about-153 violent deaths this year, including 140 homicides, with 11 ruled as self-defense and two police-action shootings. From January to June, homicides were up 55 percent in Indianapolis, but only 1 percent nationally. The year 2006 has proven to be the deadliest since 1998." (Bill Higgins, 2006, Indianapolis

Star, page E-5). All of the above problems are the cause of the breakdown of the family, kids not being nurtured by God- fearing parents.

As you can see there is a need for church religiosity to seek, and to speak to the holistic needs of the community when it comes to interpersonal relationships and getting along with others. The role of the church in the community should be to shine a bright light in the midst of despair and hopelessness. The closer we come to the heart of God through prayer the more we see our needs and the more we desire to be conformed to Christ. William Blake tells us that our task in life is to learn to bear God's beams of love. (Foster, 1978, p.30) The time to make a difference is now. The great decision makers should stand up now and be counted. Jesus has reminded the church not to be like the Pharisee saying "God, I thank thee I am not like them who lie, steal, and cheat." Many of our youth today, (black and white) have not been taught how to develop quality caring relationships. Few people have sit down with them and told them not to lie, steal, or cheat, and few have shown them how to have regard, consideration and courtesy for others. (See the character charter in back of the book) In all situations parents must teach their children to always make the extra effort to do what is right and treat others with dignity and respect. Not adhering to the law of the land will always lead to problems. The definition of crime in this regard is the violation of the criminal laws of state, the federal government, or a local jurisdiction that has the power to make such laws. (Scmalleger, 2006, p.5) Whenever a person is booked, handcuffed and charged for a crime, usually it means there was a violation of the law. A lot of African American youth are being booked for crime in cities around the country. Altogether the reason for the accelerating youth crime is the lack of the availability of employment, which affects the juvenile arrest rate. Full-time employment is associated with low arrest rates. Hereto, it also has a negative affect on public policies. The last negative affect it can have is draining the tax base of the city. Additionally in some cities people have become strangled by the fear of crime. Today in most urban schools here in America teachers have noticed that our nation is experiencing serious moral decline. Society is resorting in lying cheat, and stealing as the means of accomplishing goals. Much of the moral decay can be contributed to the breakdown of the family structure and the lack of parental guidance. Within school around the country, students lack character development. Many students are rude, impolite, and lack simple etiquette such as saying " Please and thank you " some have gone so far as to verbally attack teachers and others in the classroom. Many students arrive at school with personal problems that stem from family problems. Today is time for all forces to come together and work with our children. It is time for the business community and churches to step up to the plate to save the next generation.

Code of the Streets

Street life is all about closing the deal with those around you, and maintaining an image of toughness. It is merely about seeking out the advantageousness one has over the other. In this setting you've got to make concessions. You've got so much time and/or so much money invested in whatever it is, that the only way you can get it back is to invest in the "company of the streets" to secure what may have been lost in one way or other. This the way some hunters on the street see their lives. His whole leverage is in knowing the people around him. Someone must act as a conductor to orchestrate the efforts therefore the role of maestro falls on him as he is out on the streets. This has been their code to survival on the street, one that he must master if he is to be successful and gain a level of respect.

A well respected Sociology professor, Dr. Elijah Anderson, (1999,) of the University of Pennsylvania has this to say regarding the black male: "He offers a contemporary subculture ethnography that details the social mores that operate in some Americana inner cities today." Dr Anderson's study makes it clear that there is a street code to survival in our inner cities. He suggested the heart of the street and the issue of respect is: " Loosely defined as being treated right, being granted one's "props"(or pro due) or the deference one deserves." Out there is where he can be king and maestro. This is where he has to remain calm and upbeat when situations are particularly tense or bleak, whether he is playing chest or checkers. When under intense pressure, his palms may sweat and remain moist throughout the time of being there. He must never show any outward signs of concern or worry.

> "In the street culture, a man's sense of self-worth is determined by the respect he commands when in public. The violent nature of the street subculture, however, means that a man cannot back down from threats- no matter how serious they may be."(Schmalleger, 2004, p.233). Today's African America family places a high premium on manhood, being the head of his household and not being the man in the street, having a nine to five job, or being in business for yourself. The man was always expected to be the provider regardless of the circumstance. He is expected to be presented in the family as the strong disciplinarian. The challenge most African America males face today is their limited opportunities for legitimate success- driving many families to alternative means of money. Men who are not able to live up to the role of provider tend to abandon their mates and their children, and then may move through a series of unsuccessful relationships."
> (Schmalleger, 2004, p.223)

Therefore, we see there is a distinction from being a man in the neighborhood than being a man in the family. Today the focus must remain on being a man in the family, that's what counts more in a child's life.

What must be articulated to these men is that when one has grown beyond the stage of adolescence, he must function to the level of being able to appropriate life in such a way that people around him know and believe he is a responsible man to his family. Society defines the greatest good of a man as one who has respect from his family, and not so much from the street. The dilemma the African America male on the street finds himself in is one of identification. The self has not been defined in the person. The media and others have not defined him as man.

Street life can create an urgent addiction to the game of self-destruction centered on sex and wondering how many children he can father and how much "pussy" he can get daily.

> To many inner-city male youths the most important people in their lives are members of their peer groups. They set the standards for conduct, and to them it is important to live up to those standards, to look good in their peer's eyes. The peer group places a high value on sex, especially what middle –class people call causal sex, but though sex may be casual in terms of commitment to the partner, it is usually taken quite seriously as a measure of the boy." (Anderson, (1999, p.150)

The challenge before us is educate our girls to the game being played on the streets. There are times the young lady may be aware of what is taking place, but because she looking for someone to love she falls into play and usually ends up with the short end of the relationship.

The Community Must Go Forward

African Americans as a whole must continue to teach our youth to forge ahead in the midst of difficulty and struggle. We must teach them the value of maintaining good relationships during life. Since the 1960s there has been a breakdown of interpersonal communication skills in the black family. Father's are absent from the home at an alarming rate. The governmental Fragile Families study of Urban Parents (2006,) show African American men and women are significantly more likely to have a child by more than one partner. The study shows that 86 percent of African American fathers compared to 40 percent of white fathers, and 78 percent of African American mother compared to 46 percent of white mothers have children by one than one partner. (Carlson & Furstenberg, 2006). The issue at hand has not just began, it has its roots in racism, how the black family was separated or divided for the sake of slave labor. Often the father was sold off to another slave master. There where times the slave master would come in during the night while he was in bed with his wife and dismiss him as he impregnated his wife while children in the slave's quarters were asleep. This outrageous experience is one of the causes of the breakdown of the black family. The black male is still measured by the standard the white slave owner created.

Relationship Stage

We, as the black community can teach, describe, and model to black people the significant stages they may have to go through in order to achieve the ideal relationship when dealing with others. First, there is always positive contact. You may see the person you like and you may very well seek to join them in their space. One must always seek permission to do so, so there can be perceptual contact. They should be taught the meaning of involvement, having mutual respect for one another is important while you are seeking to learn about the other person. At this point in the relationship it is not about sex, seeking to get in bed with one another. This what is called the "initial" phase of involvement. A kind of preliminary test goes on, you can ask questions about the person, such as, "Where do you work?" "How long have you been on your job?" "Are you marry or not?" If you like the person the relationship may intensify. You can reveal more of yourself. You can share your feelings on whether you would like to see them again. If not just cut the relationship off.

Another stage is intimacy, when both partners are seeking to test one another out on how they really feel about one another. For example one my ask the other, "Tell me where you see this relationship going?" At this time you might just start talking about what you see and feel about the two of you in the future. You may come closer as friends or as a married couple. Sometimes you may joke about the future, being together as an old man or old lady. This is when you begin talking about commitment. What does it look like for the two of you? This is when the social bond begins to set in the relationship. The two of you work hard to become a unit or pair. During this time couples can show their commitment in many ways. They can become engaged and start planning to live together or agreeing to become lovers. This can be a risky time for some, because the other person may not honor their feelings, and the other party may get hurt. Below is diagram of a puzzle representing the stages of relationships and how they form in order for the relationship to maintain in positive ways. Let's examine the stages of the relationship.

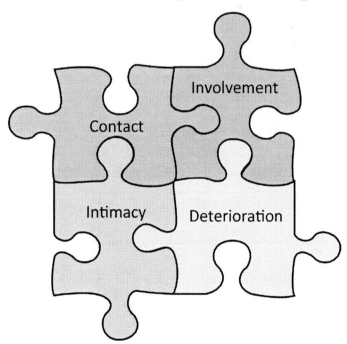

The Deterioration Stage

At this stage things can be painful. The couple may not be as close as they may have been at one time. The bond between the two of them can weaken. Getting along together may not come as easy for the two of them. There may be a personality clash in the relationship. This could be a time when one partner in the relationship may not exemplify good manners and politeness. Their demeanor may be creating a problem for the relationship. During all relationships whether it be lover or friendship, we must respond to each other in kindness and love. When you act with tact you show respect in handling a situation and all the people involved. There is always a way to provide constructive criticism without offending or hurting someone unnecessarily. The first sign of a deteriorating relationship can be when each person fails to discuss the important things in the relationship that were once important. This may be a time of dissatisfaction with everyday interaction and communication. One person could very well view the future together to be negative. The problem occurs when the dissatisfaction continues to grow in a negative manner. For example there could be a decrease in listening and talking, which may result in withdrawal in talking and self-disclose.

Interpersonal Communication during Divorce

Real love always creates, it never destroys. In this, man's only promise.
Leo Buscaglia

Agape love is always superior, it has the characteristic of God. A few years ago a friend shared with me a story which depicts the pain of divorce in the family when interpersonal communication fails between two people. Each year over a million American children suffer from the divorce of their parents; moreover, half of all children this year who live with married parents will see their parent divorce, before they turn eighteen. No matter what the age or development stage of a child, the divorce of a parent is an intensely stressful experience. Many children are inadequately prepared for the impending divorce of their parents. The beginning of a divorce is composed of a sense of vulnerability and as the family disintegrates a grief reaction to the loss of the intact family begins to create stress. This leads to a feeling of intense anger of the disruption of the family, and strong feelings of powerlessness.

I was speaking with a marriage and family counselor who spoke of the break-up and divorce of her parents. She said, "As a child I saw them fight all the time. It was frightening and heart breaking. It felt like someone had just took a knife and started cutting my flesh, blood going everywhere, as they took my heart. " Going home sometime after school was a nightmare, because I would never know if my mom would be in a good or bad mood because of my dad. She was always unhappy, crying all the time, and didn't want to take all the verbal abuse from my father anymore. He would tell her that he was sick and tired of supporting our dead asses and he would accuse her of sleeping around with guys at her job. He called her a slut and whore. As a child my relationship with my father became very weird and it felt like he was a stranger to me. Our conversation was short and frank. Later I found out that he was having an affair with another woman in a nearby city.

Watching your parents go through a divorce is not something you should go through alone. For obvious reason, for children divorce is something very traumatic. They are often concerned with their own security, not always with their parent's happiness. Children will question: "What if they leave me." "What is it that I did wrong?" "Did I cause the divorce?" "Now what's going to happen to me?" Children react in different ways with the onset of divorce. Some will be extremely sad and show signs of depression and even sleeplessness. Anxiety levels peak as they feel they are going to be abandoned or rejected by one or even both parents. Some divorce situations may make the child feel lonely. This may be due to absence of one of the parents. No matter what the situation, the child will be affected in some way by a divorce. Some children may become psychologically scarred from the experience, and still other children may not be affected emotionally at all. Much depends on how well the parents are able to handle the situation. (Fagan, 2006) Throughout this experience it is important for interpersonal communication to continue with the child and the parents.

Family structure is very important. Divorce in the family environment requires the family to restructure. Both parents must continue to play an important role in the life of their child. It is generally a good idea that the parents design a well thought out parenting plan in order to keep some predictability in the family structure. This is good for the sake of the child. Divorce does not have to mean the end of the family. It is also good for the children to keep close ties with other relatives. Even if you as the parent do not get along with the extended family, children need these people in their lives

Most parents want the best for their kids and even in the midst of their own pain, they try to help the other children get through the transition. However, some parents are so angry at their spouse, or so emotionally needy themselves, that they may put their own needs ahead those of their children, causing even more stress and potential long- term damage than the divorce itself. Here are some suggestion for parents:

- Do not argue in front of your children, bad-mouth or belittle the other parent
- Do not force the children to choose sides
- Do no blame the children for the divorce
- Do not make promises to children that you cannot keep
- Do remember that even though you are no long husband and wife and you are still parents
- Always keep the best interest of the children in the forefront
- Reassure them they are loved, that are not to blame, and are not responsible for fixing their parents
- Develop a parenting plan that allow both parents reasonable access to the children,

- Invite conversation about your child's feelings-be a good, none-defensive listener even if it's hard for you to hear, and acknowledge your child feelings whatever they are
(DeBord, 2006)

Always remember the child's need should come first. And the goal should be to maintain an interpersonal communication between you and the child.

While it is natural for children to be upset when their parents are divorcing, be aware of indications that your child may be depressed. A child's distress is most commonly seen either in acting out behaviors or in guarded, withdrawn behaviors. One sign that might indicate depression in a child is loss of spontaneity. Children are normally playful, but stress may cause a child to become morose and moody. This is usually one of the first indicators that a child is depressed, not eating problems. When depressed, some people cannot eat, while others tend to seek comfort in food and overeat, binge, or eat compulsively. Eating disorders such as anorexia or bulimia can develop as a result. If you suspect an eating problem that lasts more than a few weeks, you need professional intervention. Another is dramatic decline in grades. Sometimes children are able to find a sense of structure in their new chaotic lives by focusing on school, but if concentration is affected for an extended period, and if homework is forgotten or not completed, grades will suffer.

One of the Most Critical Issues in Divorce-the Repair Stage

To repair any relationships one must analyze what went wrong and seek to solve the problem. It is usually the behavior of one partner that causes the problem. Each can weigh the rewards and success of there relationship to determine whether they should end it or continue to work making it better and /or solve the problem. First you can ask yourself is relationship repairable or not? This is the kind of conversation both people should consider before going. This is a great time to talk about the problem, and how to correct the problem. In discussing the problem one can talk about what they are willing to do and not to do for the good of the relationship. This could be a time when both partners may be willing to seek counseling to make things better. In analyzing the relationship there are five things they can consider before repairing the relationship.

1) If the is a problem recognize it. Question what went wrong and how can we make things right. Should we try to make things better are just let them deteriorate?

2) Talk, talk-talk about the problem together ,how the two you can resolve the problem. Seek to be engage in conflict resolution. Ask your self-what kind of working strategy can you us to make thing better again.

3) Support one another- Think about what is happy times and behavior looks like. Ask yourself what are the things in the past that cause us to smile

and do those things again. Ask partner what will it take to get one another's approval again.

4) Integrate solutions to the problem. Don't just talk about the problem, if so all you will have is the problem

5) Take Risk. Give each other compliment with out any string attach .Don't wait for her/him to make the first move to say I am sorry and ask forgiveness. Always be willing to change and forgive the other partner.

Dissolution

This is the stage when both partners realize the bond of closeness is gone. The is no romance no sex, and very little contact. If you live together in the same home you may sleep in separate beds or even separate rooms. If the two of you are marriage, you may seek a legal separation and t seek out a divorce. This is usually the time when each partner seeks to avoid each other, and return to the single life. The final stage is when you began to say-good-by and you become ex-lovers and ex-friends with very little communication. During this time there can be much pain, anxiety, frustration, and sometimes guilt; because it may not turn out the way you wanted it to be

Dissolving Anger in the Black and Marriage

All relationships will experience problems. Problems are like dust in the home, at some point in life we will have it, just keep on living and breathing. People will have difference of opinions and shortcomings. Anger usually takes place in patterns and with a process. Once anger enters into the relationship partners begin to detach themselves from the other, because they may feel like their needs are not being met. They may also feel like they have not been heard and their feelings are being taken for granted. The first step in dissolving the anger is to continue to communicate: put aside one's feeling and always be willing to be in a listening mode. Listen and do not be critical. Be open and allow the other person to voice their feelings. When venting feelings we must be aware to not allow this venting to become an act of aggression which can led to outrage and disappointment. People become aggressive in relationships because of fear and frustration. When motivated by fear one often feels that their future is being threatened. In the relationship both parties must continue to keep the door open in order to continue to work together and continue to communicate.

The second process and pattern is anger and the suppression of feelings. This is a time when one person in the relationship isn't thinking smart and not placing a priority on things most important. Instead of talking about the issue they internalize the problem. Sometimes anger can be a friend and not the enemy in the relationship, it lets you know where things are going in the future. If you fail to work things out people will become angry with one another, because their unmet needs are being ignored and taking for granted. Both persons must develop a cooperative approach to their growth as individuals and as a couple. In all relationships people are always seeking to reach there potential in a loving relationship.

Obviously the root cause of all family violence lies in the accumulated anger which piles up over the years and later can lead to mental and/or physical abuse.

Main Points to Anger

1) Anger is like a smoke alarm signal or a signal of rain or storm that may be on the way in the relationship. When we become angry with one another we must find out why. Anger is a secondary emotion usually triggered by fear, low self-esteem and/or hurt feelings.

2) Anger must be acknowledged in a positive manner otherwise there will be frustration and hopelessness. Anger is a signal that lets you know that something has gone wrong and needs to be fixed. It can be likened to a car that has a flat tire or a squeak in the wheel. It can be repaired only when someone stops and fixes the damage; the tire will never fix itself. To ignore or avoid can lead to problems in other areas. What is good about anger is that it is a reliable guide that allows you to work things out to make them better.

Never avoid the issues and always discuss the problems. Both parties must continue to communicate the problems. In all relationships there must be honesty and patience. Problems don't fix themselves by themselves it takes people to work them out and to solve them.

Chapter 5
Understanding Self in Relationships

In order to be in a healthy relationship you must first have a good sense of self. You need to understand who you are and be comfortable with yourself. You must realize that the choice to be happy and whole is totally your own responsibility. Never rely on or expect others to be your source of happiness. To do this would place an undue responsibility on someone else and is an impossible task. This is why it is important not jump into relationships until we ourselves are happy and content with ourselves.

We must be aware of how our live has been shaped by life events and circumstances. Life events can have both a negative and positive affect on who we become later in life. We must come to terms with who we have become and the influences that have shaped our being. We must have a good sense of self and have the innate ability to create and be in charge of our own happiness. We must first look within. This is not to say that we can go through life alone. We do need to establish and maintain healthy relationships with others. We must realize that no man is an island and life is much more meaningful and fulfilling when shared with others.

A life disconnected from others is a life that can lead to emotional pain. When we find ourselves feeling disconnected from others we must do something about it. Remember that it is our responsibility to seek our source of happiness. Never allow the fear of rejection to dominate and take control of our being. The Scriptures make it clear and encourages the world and believers to do the same. It is written, "Consider how to stimulate one another to love and good deeds, not forsaking our own assembling together, as the habit of some, but encouraging one another in love."(Hebrews 10:24-25)

When seeking to make ourselves whole we must ask ourselves, "How is my intimacy with God? Do I spend daily time in prayer? Prayer is what connects us to the spiritual technology of God. In the book of Psalm 121 David reminds us that prayer allows us to

>Lift up our eyes to the hills from,
>whence does my help come?
>My help comes from the Lord
>Who made heaven and earth
>He will not let you foot be moved,
>He who keeps you will not slumber.
>Behold, he who keep Israel
>Will neither slumber nor sleep.
>The Lord is your keeper;
>The Lord is your shade
>On your right hand
>The sun shall not smite you by day, nor

Nor the moon by night
The Lord will keep you keep you from all evil;
He will keep your Life.
The Lord will keep your going out and coming in
From this time forward and evermore.

This is what a strong prayer life can do for an individual once there is an interpersonal relationship with Jesus Christ. This relationship can minimize emotional pain and depression. When we pray to God we release inner tensions of the heart. God is the best person to release our inner tensions to. With him we can ventilate our feelings without spreading our problems to a vast amount of people. Through prayer a person can be delivered out of trouble. The bible has often reminded us that a man that is born of a woman is of few day and full of trouble." As long as we are on top of the earth and not below it we will have disappointments, people will not always be fair during negotiations. Never forget that our troubles are not above God. Psalm 34:17-18 states "When the righteous cry for help he hears, and delivers us out of our distress and trouble." Prayer brings comfort and hope. It helps us become patient during tribulation and pain. Paul says.....knowing that tribulation worth patience; and patience, experience; experience, hope; and hope make us not ashamed; because the love of God is shed abroad in our hearts by the Holy Spirit which is given unto us." Roman 5:3 In life what precipitates stress brings on depression. Whether it the loss of a loved one or a very poor self-image. Real guilt can be a major cause of depression. Another precipitating factor of depression is that one could have a wrong perspective towards life, they can very well have wrong priorities. In life we must understand the self, the hidden self, the unknown self and blind self. The Johari window is model which explains these key principles found in the frame-like figure below. The model takes its name from its founders first names Joseph Luft & Harry Ingham. The Johari window model speaks to and represents all people in the universe, whether they are black white, Hispanic, or Native American. The Johari window represents all of us in personality. There is open side of life, those things that are open to yourself and others that you don't mind sharing and can be obvious to them when observing you as friend or foe. These are things such as your behavior, attitudes, feelings, and desires. When observing you as a person they can obviously tell whether you are a male, or female. It's those things they can openly see about you, and those things you are openly willing to share with them such as your name, age and religious affiliation.

	Known to self	Not Known to self
Known to Others	Open Self Information about yourself that you and others know	Blind Self Information about yourself that you don't know but that others do know
Not Known to Others	Hidden Self Information about your that you know but others don't know	Unknown Self Information about yourself that neither you nor others know

This diagram is commonly used for examining what you know and don't about yourself. The above diagram was take from the source Message Building Interpersonal Communication. (Devito, 2005, p.34)

Secondly, there is the blind self-area. This is usually information about yourself that you are not aware of. It could be that you are rude to only certain people when you meet them; be they female, black, or white people. An example of this point could be that when your become angry you always put your head down first. This is something others may notice about you, but you don't, it is blind to you as person.

Thirdly, there is the hidden self. It is those things that you know about yourself and you keep it from other people. It could be your personal diary of all your well guarded kept secrets. For example, what your first date to the junior prom was it like after he picked you up from your house. The hidden could be all those things you care not to reveal to your mother or father.

Fourth, there is the unknown self. This is when something is unknown to others and also unknown to you. It can be a truth that both of you don't know about you as an individual. A doctor can only reveal this truth about you when you go into this office for your yearly check up. For example, it could be you may have unrecognized talents, in some area of your life that is unknown, and it very well may be impossible to verify.

In order for the Africa America male to understand himself it is critical for him to understand himself by using the Johari Window concept. Otherwise he will always be influenced by other's opinion of him. The Johari concept will help him increase his awareness of self and others around him. It can also help one learn a great deal about themselves from a conversational point of view. This is one of the vital things that can enhance all relationships, in the family or on the everyday job experience.

Conflict Resolution from a Black Male's Perspective

"The excellent way, love, place a higher priority on relationships than on personal performance.
Communication without love becomes cold and irritating to fellow saints."
A. Charles Ware

The media often portrays black men as a group who does not know how to resolve conflict in their family and on their jobs. He is often viewed as not having a positive regard for the opponent and as having little to no ethical standards, and an inability to determine right from wrong. The black male must believe in himself and not allow someone else's opinion of him to become his reality. He must maintain confidence in himself and have the ability to hold his own.

In terms of resolving conflict the black male must become aware of the different styles of conflict resolution and the outcomes associated with each. He must show care and concern about the parties involved and not become concerned with always looking for ways for him to "win". Care must be given to never let the negotiations become a personal battle between himself and the person involved. "Many successful negotiations begin with a resounding no. But to get past that no, you must first see the possibility of yes. Once you step back and take a realistic look at what is possible, you would be surprised how often you can turn around even a seemingly no- situation." (Kolb&Williams, 2003, p.28) All conflicts will result in one of five outcomes.

1) I win, you lose-This is the competitive style that involves great concern for your own needs and desires and little for those of others.

2) I lose, you lose-This style does little to resolve conflict, it only allows it to fester and grow into resentment.

3) I lose, you win-In this style you sacrifice your own needs for the needs of the other person. It satisfies the needs of the opposition, but does little to meet your needs, which will unlikely go away.

4) I win, you win-This style addresses the needs your needs and the needs of others. This style is often considered the ideal approach.

5) Compromise –In this style I win and lose. We both give up something for the sake of the other.

The ultimate goal is to create a win-win situation for both parties. This approach takes time and willingness to communicate and especially listen to the needs of the other person. For example, I have two children a son and a daughter. Both of them ran in the house with this one large piece of candy that was given to them by a neighbor. Both children wanted the one piece of candy. They argued back and forth about who was going to get the candy. This continued until their mother came into the kitchen and cut the candy in half and gave each one a piece. This is a prime example of a win-win situation. To be successful at this time you must be a good listener and clearly hear the perspective viewpoints of each person. This style of communication will limit conflict and have very little negative consequence.

During this process of negotiation one must always seek to get all of the facts straight and in a Godly way. Seek Godly counsel through prayer. Look at creative solutions that will benefit all involved persons. The Bible says that we as believers should never enter into negotiations with contentiousness and strife, selfishness, or for unworthy ends. (Phil. 2:3, Matt. 22:39, 1Cor.13: 5 and Matt.7: 12) Be creative during the negotiation process. Look at all options before coming to a conclusion. Evaluate strengths and weakness. Never become unreasonable and always seek to be honest. Control your tongue and do the right thing for the sake of relationship.

A Black man's Tools for Negotiation

- Speak to build the other person up.
- Ask for feedback when it is needed.
- Anticipate likely reaction of the other person; always seek honety.
- Speak your words carefully.
- Seek the right time and place.
- Do not be unreasonable.
- Promote personal responsible and always be prayerful.
- Create a thought that carries the day. Have something to offer during the negotiation process. Figure out what motivates others and trade it in through the negotiation process. People are always motivated by their passion. This is what should lead you to the process of negotiation, once you figure what drives them as person or as a company. Your integrity is a very important during this time. People always like to know they can trust you to follow through with the things you promised. There are times you may not have to work at getting their trust. If you have the idea that can carry the day and that meets their needs.

Don't be surprise that reasoning and objectivity may not be a high premium at the bargaining table.

Dispositions toward conflict, biases, remembered slights or successes and the feelings that participants have about each other intruded on the personal preoccupations encroach. Dirty dishes in the sink or an impending

deadline can have more impact than frequent flyer miles on where a family decides to spend its vacation. A bargainer sure of losing ground at the office might feel obliged to take a strong stand.
 (Kolb & William, p.11)

While considering bargaining, there is nothing wrong in promoting your own interest at this time. Speak with confidence about those things that are important to you in the conversation and continue to advocate: be aware of any self –imposed limitations that you may have placed on yourself during similar experience. Learn from those experiences and continue to move being positive at all times.

The Pain of Being a Black Man in America

The black male has always been depicted as the specimen of a faulty character which has been said to be lazy, nonproductive, and ill-responsible. When you tell a person this for a long period of time, the person begins to question his capability and self worth. As a result, he falls short of his family responsibilities in some way or another. White America and the media have polarized this shortcoming as a transgression that has never been forgotten.

White America controls the world and often sets the standard for others to follow. With their birth right and status come unearned privileges due to their skin color. They create the world as they wish and nourish to their advantage. Minorities experience the pain of not having those privileges. Discrimination pushing some one out to the cave and in to the cold, because of their ethnicity or religion. This pattern is called a syllogism. Pui Yee Bery Tsang (2001) is a writer that is in touch with world around speaks of her life experience as a minority woman. Shes tell of her experience of her interracial marriage to her white husband for seven years. While in the shower, she promptly asked him a probing question "What is it like to white? " He stopped washing and replied, "Embarrassing, guilty, not very good sometimes."(Tsang, 2001, p.219-228)

One reason that people are prejudiced against one another is due to ignorance. The other reason could very well be that they have an opinion of others, but have never sat down to get to know one another. One answer is that old-fashioned racism has been replaced by a new from of racism, symbolic racism. This new form of racism represents a form of resistant to change in the racial status quo base on moral feelings that blacks violate traditional America values such as: individualism, self –reliance, the work ethic, obedience, disciple and is rooted in deep-seated feelings of social morality and in early learned racial fears and stereotypes. (Kinder & Sears 1991, p.416). The his old view still lives on today. J.B. Mc Conahay and Hough, (1997) two noted researchers argued that "blacks are pushing too much in making illegitimate demands, and that they are receiving undeserving sympathy and benefits."(p.45) Both races of people must continue work together to make this world a better place for their children, be it through school integration or on the daily job.

It's a rare day when there's good news about the lives of Black men. Countless articles tell us that our fathers and husbands, our lovers and brothers are approaching extinction due to an unholy combination of societal ills, political misdeeds and racial wrongs. But in facing the millinium, it is imperative that we put aside the dire predictions of our early demise and get to the roots of our problems, knowing them, we can solve them. African Americans are already committed to programs that are healing our men and our communities."

Jewelle Taylor Gibbs, a columnist in Indianapolis for The New Times, Magazine describes the polarization by the media as a false assumption, which does not reflect the record and statistics given throughout the years. She cites a 40 to 60 percent high school drop-out rate for black males as misleading. Actually, the national high school drop-out rate for black males has steadily decreased since 1960, and high school completion rates have improved dramatically. In 1970, only 54.8 percent of black males between the ages of 18 and 24 had completed high school.

In 1989, more than 72 percent have achieved this goal.

What is not fair to the black male in America is the way he is characterized and depicted. The population supports and nurtures the belief that black males are cruel to their family, particularly their wives. Ultimately they are searching for drugs and the drug peniteniary life in jail, which is the resting place for their soul.

On any given day, you can look at the television and notice the stereotypical view of the black male. Such a view grossly misrepresents the actual incidence of drug use by black youth, and it illustrates the hypocrisy of a society that views substance abuse by blacks and whites differently. Film and television generally depict the drug problem as having a black face, but according to figures from the National Institute of Drug Abuse, whites account for 80 percent and blacks for 20 percent of overall illicit drug use. While crack has been widely publicized as an inner-city problem, cocaine was in fact glamorized in the 1970s as a white, middle-class, recreational drug. (Gibbs, 1992, p.11)

During the 1960-1980's, the record indicates that not all black males were addicted to drugs, nor were they gang members. In 1990, criminal justice authorities released the alarming statistics that one of every four black males ages 20 to 29 were involved in the criminal justice system-in jail, on probation, or on parole. Although some critics have questioned the accuracy of these figures, one very important statistic has gone unnoticed in the debate: Three of every four young adult black males are not involved in criminal behavior. Moreover, juvenile justice experts have pointed out that black youth tend to be arrested, booked, convicted and incarcerated at higher rates than white youth who are committing similar crimes.(Gibbs, 1992, p.11)

If a black male is walking down the street and a crime has occurred, the first person law officials will attack is the black male. Black men are victims of crimes and injustices. Today, what would rid us of the stereotypical views of one another is for us to work together as people, not as blacks and whites. Such a relationship would bring about authentic character and love for us all.

The Role of the Church in the Black Family

Many blacks today attribute their success to their strong belief in God and their church. The church has been more than a place of worship for the black family. It has been a place Lord, of love and peace, a place to find serenity and tranquility, free from the world's agitation. Many of the songs which are sung during the worship service speak to the black struggle in history, songs such as the traditional "Freedom Train a-Comin":

> Hear that-a freedom train a-coming, coming, coming,
> Hear that freedom train a-coming, coming, coming,
> Hear that freedom train a-coming, coming, coming,
>
> It'll be carryin' nothing but freedom, freedom, freedom
> Get on board, oh, oh, get on board.
> It'll be carryin' freedom fighters, fighters, fighters
> Get on board, get on board.
> It'll be carryin' registered voters, voters, voters
> Get on board, get on board.

It'll be rollin' through Mississippi, Mississippi,
Mississippi
Get on board, get on board.
Author Unknown

Another favorite traditional tune is "I Want Jesus to Walk With Me:"

I want Jesus to walk with me; I want Jesus to walk with me; I want Jesus to walk with me; All along my pilgrim journey, Lord, I want Jesus to walk with me.

In my trials, Lord, walk with me; In my trials, Lord, walk with me; When my heart is almost breaking, Lord, I want Jesus to walk with me.

When I'm in trouble, Lord, walk with me; When I'm in trouble, Lord, walk with me; When my head is bowed in sorrow, Lord, I want Jesus to walk with me.

Author Unknown

The black worship service is considered one of the most diverse forms of worship. Some black churches are very staunch in their ways while others are spiritually motivated and truly sing and give praises to God. Many of its members beccome totally involved with the service, because it is a time for true celebration. Celebration can be done by saying "Amen" to the preaching of the gospel and by clapping to the sounds of the gospel music. These praises are given to God because "God so loved the world that he gave his only begotten Son" (John 3:16). It was because of this love that people of color were delivered from the oppressions of yesteryear and from the yoke of racism today. Black Americans must not forget their culture and the ways in which their foreparents worshiped. Black Americans should energetically use their voices to sing praises to God. In order to really appreciate this style of worship, one must understand the history of black Americans. Worship is celebrating the grace of God for bringing the black family out of slavery to where it is today. It is very much likened to Joshua and the walls of Jericho. When the wall was up, blacks were not allowed to function in society as a total human being. The wall "came a tumblin' down" with the passage of the Voter's'Right Act in 1965.

During slavery, the church was the only real emotional oulet for black Americans. This was the only place where our black ancestors could be among themselves and sing praises to God for allowing them to come as far as they had come. They prayed and asked God to continue to deliver them from evil and to keep them strong. It was only at church that many black Americans could start to feel good about themselves and start having hope that a change would come. After the end of slavery, the church instilled social change into the hearts and minds of black Americans. It was at church that they learned to better their conditions and to help others less fortunate. The advantages of education and knowledge were taught. In today's time the church is still considered a "shelter from a stormy past."

During the black worship service, it is not unusual for the minister to pray for economic justice for all humankind. The minister may pray that all humankind would remove the chains of oppression and the yoke of injustice from all the oppressed people. One of the central focuses is on liberation theology, allowing men and women of color to fall from the hills of oppession and to rise to the mountains of literacy by opening the doors of education and knowledge. If the black church is truly committed to the needs of its members, it must present racial programs and the minister must preach social change.

The church has always been central to the black existence. It is the place where we as a people found our strength for the following week. Most blacks have grown up with a deep sense of spiritual belief in the presence of God in their life. It is that presence which helps blacks to cope with the struggles they may face as a family.

The great black writer, E. Franklin Frazier, describes the black church as a "refuge in a hostile white world."(Frazier, 1974, p.59) Even today it is a place of strength for the black family. The strength comes from listening to God's Word and listening to and hearing the preached word which often reminded its people that God will make a way out of no way--just wait and see the salva-tion of the Lord.

Out of the working of the black church came strong prophetic leaders. Nat Turner lived during the time of slavery during the 1800's. David Walker spoke to the appeal of the colored citizens of the world. He spoke to the conscience of America to abolish slavery as a practice not in line with the scriptural principles of the Christian faith. Dr. Martin Luther King is the leader most of us are familiar with today. He challenged all persons to love one another regardless of skin color and heritage. These are just a few blacks who have emerged out of the pews of the black church to a high level of creativity, reminding all of us as a people of this world that we all are family, made in the image of God.

The black church has been a strong mechanism within the black family throughout history. It is in the church where many of its parishioners found the emotional tools of learning. Many of the black schools such as Wilburforce University in Ohio, Morris Brown College in Atlanta, Morehouse College in Atlanta, and Tuskegee University in Tennesee, and a host of other schools which are not mentioned, originated from the struggle of the black church.

Blacks could not attend white colleges and universities due to segregation so these schools were formed as a way of strengthening the black family. The schools, elementary, secondary, and those which provided the beginnings of college maintained a religious and moral outlook. The graduates of these schools went forth as missionaries to raise the moral and religious level of the members of their race. Many of the men were preachers or became preachers.(Frazier, 1974, p.45)

The schools were also assisted through funds from white missionaries. The black clergy were often the first persons to become educated within the ranks of its people. Through the education of the clergy came a major thrust of political involvement as a people, challenging people to vote so they could have a voice in the community they lived in. The black church and the black family have always worked together in strengthening themselves as a race of people.

We have allowed our doctrine of the church in the black tradition to emerge out of the context. The extended family has been employed as a way of imaging the black church. Since our goal has been to make these two primary black institutions mutually supportive, it has been proper to use the family image in reference to a black ecclesiastic. Since black families are the source of the black church's life and growth, the measure of its ministry to black families will determine the quality of its own mission.(E.Franklin. Frazier, 1957, p.45)

The church is known to be the paradigm of hope and inspiration to the black family. They both share the commonality of racism and oppression. Within this commonality, there arises the struggle to succeed as a people within the black community. The black church cannot dismiss itself from the struggle of its blackness, because to address the black need and its family need the black church must understand and speak to the needs of its people. The black church emerged out of the struggle to be free.

The church is family. Slavery did everything humanly and satanically possible to destroy the black family. The church kept the concept of family alive. God was the parent, but those who gathered came together as a few of God's "helpless children." As God's children, blacks understood the nature of the church to be the performance of these rituals which cemented family members to each other and to God. (Scott, 1985, p.17)

The mission of the black church is to reach those within its community and those who are a part of the struggle. "The Black church has traditionally relied upon a preached theology. Now that era may be past. The Blacks of this generation, and possibly for generations to come, are going to write their own theology in the light of their circumstances and need."
(Scott, 1985, p.17)

The black pastor holds a unique image within the context of the black church. He or she is a vision of hope, a prophet, politician, teacher, father, and mother. He or she is a mother in the sense that he or she has been the nurturing force on which the vision of his or her people depend. Without his or her spiritual direction and love, his or her people would lack the social transformation of society, which is part of his or her thrust as a prophet challenging America to live out his or her true creed and justice for all humankind. His or her vision is a vision of assurance for black people, a vision of love and hope. The black church really believes and supports the belief that without a vision they will perish. The black pastor always has a vision for his or her people. This vision is embodied in the pastor first and then in his or her people. Without the pastor the black church would not be on the forefront speaking to the conscience of America. Because of his or her high visibility as a leader, the black pastor has always been the politician and speaker for the house. Parishioners within the church look for his or her spiritual leadership to make a difference within the community. Edward P. Wimberly, (1987) a noted Black theologian from International School,of Theology, in Atlana Georgia quoted Cornwall (1987) saying:

> The black pastor has been expected, as a symbol of the community, to help the person in crisis find meaning for his or her existence. Often the expectation has been that the pastor would provide specific advice and direction to the person. In some instances, the pastor was expected to take over and take charge. This taking-over function is called parenting.(p.17)

This is the dilemma that the black United Methodist Church is facing. The black church has always relied upon the strong leadership of the pastor in history. When the central jurisdiction (black churches) merged with the Methodist Church (white congregations) in 1968 in Dallas, Texas, some of the cohesiveness that the black church had as a people was taken away. They had to rely upon the structure of the white inclusive church, whereas the black church in history had always relied upon the strength of its people and its leaders. The black chuch has not so much relied upon the vision of the pastor, but upon the vision of the white church. This has been a shortcoming as a black people. All people must work together to create a vision of social change within the black community and within the white community. The black pastor is more than just a pastor in the church. He or she is a role model to many that do not have a father present in the home. This is part of the uniqueness of the black church. People in the black church provide the nurture that is part of the struggle of being black growing up in America.

In this church environment, oppressed blacks will find others who share in the commonality of oppression. As the nuclear family in all its brokenness comes to the church, it finds a place where surrogate mothers and fathers, brothers and sisters, uncles and aunts are willing to receive them and adopt them into their fold.(Scott, 1985, p.28) This is one of the unique characteristics of the black family within the church. It offers strength to the motherless and hope for the fatherless

APPENDIX (1)

How would define your relationship with the one you love?

1) Discuss your relationship with your Mother .
2) Discuss your relationship with your Father.
3) Do black women have different way of communicating than White women?
4) Have you ever been angry with the one you love?
5) What does mean to be a black male in America?
6) Discuss the role of a mother/father in the family?

Appendix (2)

The Stage of Marriage
For pastoral use only
For Discussion

The Honeymoon Period:

A) Excited that they met one another
B) Looking forward to the future
C) Seeking to please

Romantic Period:

A) Each partner is at there best
B) Negative faults are overlooked

Early Marriage:

A) Reality of life begin to se-in
B) Reality of day- to day living

Full Stage Reality (Critical Stage)

A) Job pressure (relocating, demands on the family time ect.)
B) Different opinions on family finances
C) Obligations and conflicts with child rearing
D) Time pressure
E) Blended Families

Rejection

Death of the relationship
A) Emotional divorce
B) Legal divorce

The loss of a love one in Marriage
For pastoral used only

1. When we lose a love one, be it through long- term illness, by death, or by an extended separation, we usually go through various stages. These stage include:

    A. Shock
    B. Worried feelings
    C. Believing things will never be the same
    D. Grief/ guilt
    E. Remembering the past (happier occasion)
    F. Releasing of intensity (angry, frustration, denial)
    G. Acceptance (finding ways to go on with life; dealing with the lose: accepting reality)

H. Giving them up (going on with your life).

3. Continuing the Promise
4. Do we drop out?
5. Do we make up?
6. Time to review life
7. Realizing that there is hope for the future, crossing the river-that is moving on.

BIBLIOGRAPHY

Andrew Billingsley, Black Families in White America (Prentice-Hall, Inc., 1968), p. 3.

Bales Kevin , Disposable people. New Slavery in the Global Economy, Revise Edition, University of California Press 2oo4, ISBN O-520-24384-6 Slavery-Wikipedia the Free Enclopedia Htt: // enwikipedia. Org/ wiki/Slavery Retrieval Date September 12, 2006

Caron F.Strong Mother-Strong Sons- Raising Adolescent boy in the '90s Henry Holt and Company NewYork, p,42 1994

Destroying Black Boys," Essence (November 1989), p. 55. (Prentice-Hall, Inc., 1968), p. 3.

Engel Beverly Excerpts from The Emotionally Abusive Relationship: How to stop Being Abuse and How to Stop Abusing 2002 Reprinted with permission of John Wiley& Son, inc.

CBS Evening New Document on Violent Crime in the Mid-Cities.www.News.com Retrieved on Octerber 17,2007 Focus on Kids :The Effects of Divorce on children.www.ces.ncsu.edu Retrieved on October 11, 2006.

David J. Dent, "Readin', Ritin' and Rage: How Schools Destroying Black Boys," Essence Magazine (November 1989), p. 55.

Devito A.Joseph (2005) Messages Building Interpersonal communication skills. Person Education Inc. 6.Edition NewYork.Boston

Fagan, Patrick. The effects of Divorce.www.hertiage. org Retrieved on at 7.05 October 11, 2006.

Higgins, Bill, Indianapolis Star News Crime Report, December 2006

Foster Richard J Celebration of Discipline the Path to Spiritual Growth Harper& Row, Publishers New York, Hagerstown,San Franciso, London, 1978 p. 30

Gibbs, JewelleTaylor, " Media Myths About Black Men," The New Times February 1992

Judson Cornwall, Unfeigned Faith (Fleming H. Revell Company, 198 1), p. 62.

J. Deotis Roberts, Roots of a Black Future: Family and Church (The Westminister Press, 1980), pp. 24-25.

David J. Dent, "Readin', Ritin' and Rage: How Schools

Destroying Black Boys," Essence (November 1989), p. 55. J. Deotis Roberts, Roots of a Black Future: Family and Church (The Westminister Press, 1980), pp. 24-25.

Destroying Black Boys," Essence (November 1989), p. 55. (Prentice-Hall, Inc., 1968), p. 3.

Kinder, D R. and D.O Sears. 1991 " Prejudice and politics: Symbolic Racism versus Racial Threats to the Good Life" Journal of Personality and Social Psychology 40,414-431.

Kottler Jeffrey Taking Responsibility with Blaming :A New way of Resolving Conflicts in Relationships, Copy @ 1994 by Jossey- bass Inc.p, 505 Researched from Bridges not Walls A book about interpersonal communication ninth edition John Stewart Publish by McGraw- Hill New York, Ny, 2006

Lavelle Kristen is a doctor student at Texas A& M University and does research on white antiracist . htt: proquest. Uni.com. indianapolis libproxy.ivty. edu.Retreival Date 9/29 2006

Linda& Richard Eyre Teaching your children values Fire Simon& Schust Building Rockefeller Center NewYork, NY 10020 .p 93.1993

Metropolitan School District of Washing Townshop.(1998). Washing Township Saturday School Program Hand Book(Available from Washington Township Schools)Indianaplois, In 46240

McConahay,Jb.,and J.C Hough, Jr. 1976. Symbloic Racism. Journal of Social Politic 45,

The New Times (February 1992), p Martin L. King Strength to love Harper & Row edition published June 1963 New york . New york . 1st printing.

P.Y. B. Tsang . "There's a white Man in My Bed" Talking about Identity ed. By Carl Jame and Adrienvve Shadd, pp. 219-228 Copy @ 2001 Reprinted by permission of Between the Line Toronto.

Wallace Charles Smith, The Church in the Life of the Black Family (JudsonPress, 1985), p. 32

Wheat, Ed & Gloria Okes Perkins, Love life for Every Marriage Couple Zondervan Publishing House, 1990,

Dr. Wilcox, Professor at the University of Virginia, PowerPoint Presentation in Chapel Hill, SC in

September 2006, Sponsored by the government on strengthening the black family

William Strickland, "Black Men In Crisis," Essence November 1989),p.49

Wallace Charles Scott, The Church in the Life of the Black Family (Judson Press, 1985), p. 17.

Printed in the United States
75583LV00001B